THE DRILL SERGEANT'S GUIDE TO PARENTING

PRAISE FOR STEVEN J THOMPSON

"Thompson, AKA Drill Sergeant Dad, writes it as he tells it as he sees it. But beneath that brim hat he also has a heart. A very fun and insightful read (even for this former Air Force brat)."

— Eric Miller, Blogger (www.etcguy.com), author, and freelance writer for Hockey Player Magazine

"From the first paragraph, I couldn't put it down. I laughed, bristled, cringed, nodded, reminisced, read sections out loud, shook my head and laughed again. Thompson's Drill Sergeant's Guide to Parenting is informative and poignant, and what we need hear in today's culture. I recommend it to parents of all ages."

— Ken Young, author of "The King's Frog Hunter"

ALSO BY STEVEN J THOMPSON

The Daughter's Daring &
The Enchanted Forest

The Daughters Daring & The Crystal Sea

THE DRILL SERGEANT'S GUIDE TO PARENTING

STEVEN J THOMPSON

KECELJ PUBLISHING

Copyright © 2019 by Steven J Thompson

All rights reserved.

Print ISBN: 978-0-9967232-4-4

Edited and Formatted by Edits By Stacey

Cover Art By Jane Dixon-Smith

The views and opinions expressed in this book are those of the author and do not in any way reflect the official policy or position of Army Drill Sergeants or the United States Army. Anyone who takes it that way is being an asshole.

No part of this book may be reproduced in any form or by any electronic or mechanical means, including information storage and retrieval systems, without written permission from the author, except for the use of brief quotations in a book review.

For R. Lee Ermey

DRILL SERGEANT CREED

I am a Drill Sergeant
I will assist each individual in their efforts to become a highly motivated, well disciplined, physically and mentally fit soldier, capable of defeating any enemy on today's modern battlefield.

I will instill pride in all I train.

Pride in self, in the Army, and in country. I will insist that each soldier meets and maintains the Army's standards of military bearing and courtesy, consistent with the highest traditions of the U.S. Army.

I will lead by example, never requiring a soldier to attempt any task I would not do myself. But first, last, and always, I am an American Soldier. Sworn to defend the Constitution of the United States against all enemies, both foreign and domestic. **I am a Drill Sergeant.**

INTRODUCTION

Hey You! Thanks for checking out my book. I appreciate my readers, and I hope you find this guide helpful. That's probably the last nice thing I say to you for a few chapters. If you don't like it go fuck yourself.

This guide is not about sugarcoating anything. It's an opinionated guide for new, soon to be, or even veteran parents. You've heard the phrase "in my humble opinion?" Well not here. My opinions are not humble. I spent ten years as an Army Reserve Drill Sergeant training tomorrow's soldiers for the rigors of battle, and I did not get them out of bed at 0430 every morning by asking them nicely. Nor was I humble.

I sometimes use colorful language and references in this guide. For those of you who went to public schools that means I cuss some. I do try to limit the use of the "F" word, but shit happens so brace yourself. If you are offended by any of my opinions on parenting, stop and ask yourself why you're so offended? Then take a deep breath and move on to the next section. Just remember you are always welcome to go fuck yourself.

In this guide, I give you my opinion on the best ways to

Introduction

raise your kids. Not only have I served in the world's finest military, but I am the father of three awesome children spanning from ages fourteen to twenty. My kids are healthy and happy. They have never seen the back seat of a police car, the back room of an abortion clinic, or the dirty mattress of a crack house. They are not overweight or emotionally disturbed, but they are all deadly accurate with a high-powered rifle.

While I'm not a licensed family therapist, I am trained and practiced at turning young people into well-rounded adults. You are welcome to take or leave anything I say in this guide. None of it is gospel, and I don't need your validation to feel better about myself. In fact, I hope you tell the whole world what a total asshole I am, so long as you and they buy this book. But if you do find it helpful, I'm happy to see you share it with your friends. If more parents in this great nation did a better job of raising their kids, we could eliminate the need for a lot of expensive social services in this country.

A good friend once told me that success is not an option. When you make the choice to make success your only outcome, you will succeed. Sometimes it will not be a success by the standards of others, and that's just fine. Make your own goal of what success looks like and stick to it.

Ultimately, I do hope you follow this guide and that it helps you raise your kids. Parenting is a tough job, and we could all use a guidebook sometimes. This is a job that I very much want you to succeed at, and it's OK to not go it alone. Even Drill Sergeants needs a battle buddy.

And finally, one more time. If any you find any of this material disagreeable or offensive, you are welcome, at any time, to GO FUCK YOURSELF! Hooah!

YOUR MISSION, SHOULD YOU CHOSE TO ACCEPT IT.

There was Joe Snuffy, not even a Private in the Army yet, sitting down and pigging out on that Whopper with fries the weasel-fucking recruiter had bought him. Visions of Ranger tabs and Airborne glory danced in his head, but little Joe Snuffy was destined to be a short order cook, because his recruiter had a weird quota to fill that month, and he just didn't like the little pimply-faced moron anyways.

First off, if you're one of my former privates, let me just stop you right here. Go look in a mirror numskull. Does the world really need a carbon copy of your ugly pie smasher? What makes you think you are qualified at this station? Did you actually find a spouse, partner, or significant other willing to make a baby with your dumbass?

Now, if any of you are not my former trainees and you are actually reading this *before* you made a baby, bravo! Give yourself one last pat on the back. Feel good? Outstanding. Now ask yourself, what makes you so damn qualified for this? Private Joe Snuffy can apply a field bandage, qualify with an M-16, AND sleep standing up! But his dumb ass sure isn't ready for no baby, so why are you? Do yourself and the free world a favor by taking the strongest birth control known to man. Yes, I mean you need to babysit someone else's kids. One night should do it. Or go down to Chuck E Cheese and sit for five minutes. Trust me, you'll run screaming to the nearest liquor store.

Alright, so if you did that and you're still convinced, let's ask you some more preliminary questions to make sure you can handle the task at hand. Again, this is assuming you haven't already made a baby (or two or three) which is a bad assumption on my part. But let's just entertain the notion that you're one of the smart ones who listened to your parents before you went and got knocked up. Even if you have already made children, these little questions will hopefully convince you to become a more responsible parent.

Let's start with some obvious but often overlooked points, like ***"Hey Asshole! Do you have a job?"*** How about a means of supporting yourself and your future offspring that doesn't involve my tax dollars? Private Joe Snuffy has a job. He serves in the world's finest military and defends your freedoms so that you can go down to the hippie health center and munch granola in peace. What's your job? Babies don't just come equipped with diapers, and formula like a GI Joe action figure comes equipped with a plastic rifle and Kung Fu grip. You have to freaking buy that stuff, hero!

If you do not have a job or a means of real support, you should check yourself right now. Kids cost money. A lot of it. Minimum wage is barely enough to support yourself, let alone kids. Ask yourself why you want to have kids when you're not financially ready. Then go to school and get a better job. If you come from a wealthy family and have a huge trust fund, good for you, but go get a job anyway and learn how the rest of us live, hippy.

How you support yourself leads to the next question.

Exactly WHO are you going to make a baby with? Are you married? If not, that is highly advisable before you make babies. The next option is what we civilized Americans used to call a shotgun wedding. For Private Snuffy that literally means your new father in law forces (with threat of violence) you to marry the young *lady* (questionable term here) that you went and knocked up!

For you fellows out there, think of this. Why do you want to make babies with this female? Is she intelligent (also questionable if she is with you)? Does she know how to make a home, cook dinner, and balance a bank account? Is she terrible at all these things, but her daddy is rich? Wake up chowder head! I can't tell you how many young men I have counseled who ended up paying child support for a child they no longer are allowed to raise because they made a baby with a woman who they thought was the cat's freaking meow the first two weeks of their so-called relationship! If you took the time to date her a couple times first (third time is usually the charm) to see if any signs of crazy vindictive bitch come out, you would know better than to sign over half of your future earnings to her!

Now, as this is the modern world and I am an equal opportunity offender, ahem, Drill Sergeant, I am going to counsel you young female types as well. Since you are the ones left carrying the future diaper destroyers for nine months, you may want to pay close attention. You see, I get it. I really do. Even though I look at Private Snuffy and see a zit-faced DNA stain that possibly escaped the psyche ward, I realize that some of you young females see a handsome, suave, Don-freaking-Juan Demarco of the ever-loving trailer park or ghetto of your wildest dreams! At least he bought you enough shots of Fireball to convince you to get frisky with him in the back of his grandma's Buick.

I'm asking you ladies to consider a few things here. Does

the Private Snuffy of your dreams have a JOB? Notice how I emphasize jobs here a lot. That's because our beautiful country already has enough damn welfare babies! Beyond that, does he dress appropriately? If his pants sag down past his butt and he has a tattoo on his freaking neck (or anywhere else above the neckline), you should drop his ass like a hot potato, sister. If you follow my rule of dating him three times and you start to suspect that he's a lazy, bed-wetting hippie, or worse, an abuser of women, drop his ass at the nearest Marine recruiting center and tell them he said all marines are limp wristed cheese weenies. That should do the trick.

Now, if either of you males or females are considering raising children on your own (by choice, not just because you shared DNA with a total douchebag)? Hold that thought. I've got some choice words for your dumbass in chapter two. Just be patient, Einstein.

If the rest of you have made it this far and you still want to trade your skinny jeans and hot rods for pastels and minivans, good for you. America needs more potential taxpayers, producers, and warriors. However, we need fewer criminals, crackheads, and telemarketers so you'd better get this right.

Having children is not a mission that you should take lightly. Sure, lots of people are doing it, but many aren't doing it very well. Your parents probably made it look easy; not that this stops you from criticizing their parenting skills and telling yourself how you're going to do it so much better, right? Wrong. Odds are you'll just turn into your parents, Genius. For most of you, that's not such a bad thing. They raised you after all, and now you see yourself as so fucking special that you want to make little copies of yourself!

But here's the wakeup call, soldier. The reality check. Are you ready? This one's a doozy. The truth is, once you have children, IT'S NO LONGER ALL ABOUT YOU, JERKWAD!

The Drill Sergeant's Guide to Parenting

You see, once you have children, you're now the parent. You're the one who's responsible, and unless America's left-wing politicians legalize extreme late-term abortion for two-year-olds (for the environment, of course), there's no turning back from this one. There's no return policy for children, and if you break it, you and society will pay.

So, say goodbye to sleeping in. Say goodbye to the carefree life you used to live. Say goodbye to crazy three-day parties filled with sex, drugs, and rock n roll. Those days are behind you. You're in my world now chump. Being a parent is a lot like being a drill sergeant, and you don't get the option of quitting. At least not until you accomplish your mission of raising your offspring and sending them out into the world.

Your decisions from here on don't just affect you. They affect your children too. They affect the rest of your family when you start screwing this up and they have to stand in for you. They also affect the rest of society when your little monster takes their anger for you out on everyone else.

Don't believe me? Look at our nation's prisons. They're filled with young men who grew up without fathers. Our welfare rolls? Yup. Filled with single moms who made some really poor choices. Do I believe in second chances? Sure, but the world would be a lot better place if so many of you wouldn't screw it up so bad the first time!

If you've really given this some thought, if you've weighed all of your options, if you've chosen a mate who you're ready to partner with on life's greatest journey, then let's do this (NO, not you and me chowder head). By let's, I mean you. Go light some candles, ingest your favorite brand of hooch, and get to baby-making soldier! Report back to me at 0400 hours with a progress report! Wait, scratch that. Just call your doctor or your mommy. Fucking weirdo.

* * *

WHAT YOU WILL NEED

Now here's the good news. You're not the first to try this. In fact, dumber people than you have been raising babies for thousands of years now. The majority of them were also not raised in the greatest nation in the history of mankind, so you have a distinct tactical advantage. Still, there are some things you will need to do this job right.

Probably the first thing you really need is **confidence**. Babies are scary, but you have to believe that you can do this. As your children grow, they will figure out if you're unsure of yourself. I have to stress this very firmly: YOU ARE THE ONE WHO IS IN CHARGE. When I meet new trainees for the first time, I let them know that I am a Drill Sergeant and their asses belong to me. There is no democracy; only my authority. You can never leave any room for doubt on this matter.

You see, conflict in our world is not caused by hatred or greed so much as by the uncertainty of just who the fuck is in charge. Throughout history there have been many nations that were unsure of who was in charge, and so they started some shit, much like Japan and Germany once did with the U.S. In response, we lit their asses up like the 4th of July and made sure they knew, in no uncertain terms, that we were the HMFIC's.

Your children can, at times, be like Japan and Germany (I've heard some parents refer to them as insurgents). As long as they know you are absolutely in charge, they will generally behave well. Occasionally though (OK, often), they will try to test this authority, and you will have to rain down on them like holy hellfire.

Authority is not the same thing as cruelty. We do not punish our children for the sake of being mean. Our actions are meant to teach them that there are consequences to their decisions. Many drill sergeants have adopted the phrase "polite, but firm." This is a good phrase for you to consider as well. Sometimes a child needs a good spanking to correct their behavior. They do not, however, need you to beat them with a stick or throw them against walls. Control your anger or someone with more authority than you will step in and control it for you, asswipe.

There are also times when you let them learn their own lessons. Because basic training is short and loaded with a lot of tasks, a Drill Sergeant doesn't have time to let privates learn a lot on their own. As a parent, you have years. You don't always have to save your kids from their own mistakes. If they leave their sweater outside in the rain, let them learn what it means to have a soaking wet sweater, and see if they figure out how to use the damn dryer on their own.

You need **knowledge**. Knowledge can come from pre-parenting classes, talking to other parents, or reading guides like the one in your grubby mitts right now. Knowledge of any given subject is what gives us the confidence to make decisions with authority. Drill Sergeants are not allowed to lead troops until they demonstrate their knowledge of their basic tasks and drills. For example, you should already have the knowledge that playing in traffic would be bad for your soggy-diapered insurgents. With this knowledge, you can act with total confidence in your command decision to lock their asses behind a damn fence (or baby gate for you suburban types). Now think of some other dangerous situations for your offspring and apply the same principles. Too easy.

Where do you get the knowledge to raise kids? Well, the library (or Amazon) is full of books on parenting, including this one. You're probably too proud to ask your parents, but try some of your friends' parents. And what do you need knowledge of? Like how often should you take your kid for doctor checkups? The dentist? How about local school districts? Do you know how safe your home is for little kids? This is all knowledge that you need, and you will feel a lot more confident once you have it. In the Army, this would be referred to as battlefield intelligence. Know your operating environment so that it doesn't give you a nasty surprise.

You will also need **patience**. Patience comes from knowledge and confidence. Someone who is unsure of themselves will lose their shit a lot faster than someone who knows what's up. If Japan and Germany are testing you on international waters, just be patient. However, if they roll a tank across our southern border, you need to destroy that target with extreme prejudice. It also helps to have the knowledge of what is one step too far for them and what is too extreme of a reaction from you. When in doubt, take complete charge of any situation. Always maintain your command presence. Own that shit mama!

This does not imply that you have to yell at your kids. OK, I'm guilty. I yelled at my kids sometimes just as I yelled at the trainees. It's often necessary with trainees because there's fifty of them mulling around and I need them all to hear me, but I didn't have fifty kids, and hopefully neither do you. When you yell at your kids too often, they start to tune it out. Try leaning in and whispering to them about the horrible fate about to befall them if they don't knock their shit off. How about "I know where you sleep, and I will shave your eyebrows." I have found that whispering can be scary for them and personally rewarding for you!

Drugs & Alcohol

Just a little side note about your choice of recreational

substances. I probably shouldn't have to bring this up, but if you've seen any reality TV show you know I have to. Once you have kids, you need to put away recreational drugs completely. Women shouldn't be using any once they're pregnant, and you men should give it up as well. You can't very well parent when you are stoned or in jail, knuckleheads. If you happen to be from California or Colorado, you might think marijuana is OK, right? Wrong. Marijuana might not be morally wrong, but it comes with a lot of illegality and social disdain. It could very well be a wonder drug for you, and I'm sure there are parents who balance this, but if it's something you need for your maladies, you might not be in the best position to parent. Can you honestly put it down? If not, you've got some serious thinking to do.

At the risk of being a hypocrite (being a parent is a fucking license to be a hypocrite, btw) I'm going to tell you that alcohol is a slightly different situation. Mostly because it's legal. It still has the potential to ruin your life and your children's' lives, but it's a little easier to handle if you self-regulate. I make the exception for alcohol because every now and then parents need to unwind. Sometimes dad needs a beer out in the garage, and mommy really needs some wine with her friends. However, if your favorite nightly dinner soup is whiskey with ice croutons, you may have a problem. Fucking check yourself.

THE RULES

EVERY PARENT SHOULD KEEP a list of rules handy that you enforce with your children. They can be adjusted to reflect the level of dereliction of your future booger eaters.

1. I am your parent, NOT your friend. If you behave I

will let you have friends. Having parents is not optional.

2. As your parent, I have full authority over your life. To include what you wear, what you eat, and when you will sleep. Accept that this is the rule, fair or not, and your life will be easier.
3. "Do as I say and not as I do" is a perfectly good rule. If I decide to drink, smoke, and wear stripper shoes, that's my prerogative, not yours. Get over it.
4. I really don't give a shit that your friends' parents don't enforce rules like mine. Your friends will end up in a trailer park or prison. Pray I don't look too closely at them and pick new friends for you.
5. You will exercise and get some form of outdoor activity. This is for your own good and will protect you from being fat-shamed by the kids at school, or your siblings, or me.
6. Video games and TV are privileges that can be taken away. Because Fuck You.
7. Your education is not optional.
8. Dating before eighteen does not enhance your education or provide a meaningful life experience. It's a rare privilege that, short of the prom, I will likely deny you.
9. You will have a career/education plan when you turn eighteen, or I will drive you to the military recruiter myself.
10. You will respect your parents. You will also try to respect others, but always be prepared to defend yourself against those who do not respect your boundaries and well-being.
11. Special Bonus Rule (For the Airborne Ranger in the sky): If you don't like these rules you can (you guessed it) Go Fuck Yourself!

The Drill Sergeant's Guide to Parenting

You're welcome to adjust these rules to fit your household. However, I gave each of these rules a lot of thought over several beers and seeking input from at least two fellow dads and even Mrs. Drill Sergeant herself. So, your adjustments will probably suck.

PARENTING IS A TWO-PERSON JOB

There was Joe Snuffy, flowers in hand, and wearing his wrinkled Army of One T-shirt that he got from the trunk of the recruiter's car. He was down on one knee for Tammy Ray, the local trailer-park, cocktail-lounge waitress of his dreams. He was dreaming of endless fornication and increased pay for his new dependent. She just smiled thinking, this sucker's paycheck is mine...

ONE OF THE FIRST THINGS EVERYONE IN THE ARMY gets is a battle buddy. Privates have them throughout basic training. Even Drill Sergeants need them if only to have a witness when Private Snuffy does something really stupid. You need one too.

I've had this conversation with numerous people before. A lot of societal experts like to tell you that the single mom is holy, and women are awesome, and who needs a man anyway, right? Well, yes, the single mom takes on a lot, and I really do salute her efforts. But if Superman joined the army tomorrow, I'd assign him a fucking battle buddy. You need one too. That doesn't mean settling for the first loser that shows up at your doorstep. The best choices in life don't always present themselves right away, and you need to consider your kids in all of your decisions. If you can't find a partner, maybe you need grandma to come stay with you? Two parents are better than one.

The best environment for children, hands down, is a traditional married family with a mother and a father. That might not be what seems best to you, but it's what's best for them. That doesn't mean that people in other situations don't somehow make it work, because humans are able to adapt and overcome, but I'm letting you know now what the ideal standard is.

To be honest, I don't have anything against alternative parenting. If you put a roof over their heads, food on the table, and still pay your taxes, then good for you. And yes, there's a lot of traditional parents who screw it up pretty bad. However, the fact that other people screw up their kids is not an excuse for you to do the same thing. Like any traditional parents who aren't already pregnant, you should ask yourselves why you want to have kids in the first place.

Regardless of your preferences, you need a battle buddy. That doesn't mean someone you pawn the kid off on and then go drinking with your friends every night. It doesn't mean someone you take your frustrations out on. Battle buddies can be a great sounding board, but they're not your punching bag. A battle buddy is your partner and hopefully your best friend. You put your trust in each other, and you *have each other's back*. Sometimes you get pissed at each other, but you get over it and make things work.

Mission First

. . .

The Drill Sergeant's Guide to Parenting

IN THE ARMY, we do this because the mission is always more important than personal feelings. Raising your child is your mission. Always remember the phrase **mission first** and you will do fine. When you commit yourself, you rule out failure. Forget your "plan B" and your escape plan. Deal with what you have in front of you and make the best of every situation. Success is not an option.

You and your battle buddy should discuss your mission and how you plan to succeed. Do you agree on a religion for your child, or a set bedtime (not up to those of you with infants, BTW)? You need to communicate and come to an agreement on how you're going to raise your children. This is one of those pitfalls that separates a lot of couples. Even if you stay together, there's nothing worse than contradicting each other in front of your children.

Can you imagine Drill Sergeants contradicting each other? If I tell the privates to march one click north, but Drill Sergeant Jones comes along and tells them its two clicks south, we might have a problem here. OK, total disclaimer for Private Snuffy's sake; yes, we actually do contradict each other, but mostly because it's freaking hilarious to watch all the Joe Snuffies wandering around confused. But you shouldn't do that with your children unless you need a good laugh. Then sometimes it's OK.

Communication is also key with battle buddies. Let's face it, this is a tough job. Sometimes we get frustrated with the way things are going, and children, like privates, are such an easy target to take out our anger. Believe it or not, a good Drill Sergeant doesn't spend every waking hour just yelling at their troops, and neither should you as a parent. If you see your battle buddy having a rough time, you need to pull them aside, ask what's bothering them, and help solve the problem. They might just need someone to talk too. They also might take it out on you, but better that than your child. They'll thank you later.

A battle buddy also helps answer a serious question you hope you'll never have to ask. Who is going to take care of your child if something happens to you? See, you may think you can just go it alone, but when you bring little people into the equation, it's about more than just your ego. Do you trust your parents to step in and raise your children if you die tomorrow? You might want to write this down. You might just want to have a plan in place for this shit.

Things You Should Agree On

Aside from financial planning and extramarital affairs, disagreements on raising children are one of the big issues that separate parents. If your parents were strict, that's probably what you will want to do. But what about your partner? They may have come from a more lenient family. Parents range from the overprotective to the completely oblivious of their children, so this is something you need to discuss.

You need to agree with your partner on basic rules and then stick to them. If 9:00 pm is bedtime, then stick to that rule. Children, like privates, feel safer when there is discipline in their lives. When you take that discipline away, you leave them feeling insecure and unsure of themselves. So, letting them eat candy at midnight might seem fun, but (trust me on this) it's a really bad idea that will backfire. The grandparents give your kids candy for a lot more sadistic reasons than you might think. Hint: It's revenge for all the stupid fucking shit you did in their household!

Regardless of your religion, you also need to discuss what

value system you will be teaching your children. I believe you should teach them that America is the greatest fucking nation in the history of mankind, that God and guns saved the free world, and that hard work purifies the soul. If you're more of the belief that America is an oppressive nation, that guns should be outlawed, and that work is for suckers who don't know how to fill out welfare forms, well, I think you might better enjoy raising your kids in Canada, or Russia, or Stinkyshitastan. Knock yourself out, hippy.

IF YOU DIVORCE

IN LIFE, there is always the exception to the rule (or the Drill Sergeant who is just badass enough to break it), and this is no exception. When you play house with another adult, regardless of how special you thought it was, it might someday come to an end. Or in Private Snuffy's case, I freaking told you if you married that stripper with a coke addiction it was going to end badly!

Sometimes marriages, or partnerships, or whatever you freakos are calling it these days, end. The first thing you need to do (after getting shit-faced drunk and sleeping with their best friend) is find a way to part amicably and as adults. Ladies, do not go straight to a lawyer looking for ways to keep your children from their father. That punishes your kids as well as him, and one day they'll know what you did and hate you for it. Gentleman, you can lawyer up, but unless you've got pictures of her in the back seat of Private Snuffy's grandma's Buick, you're pretty much screwed. Hope you didn't marry a complete psychotic bitch. If you're in the infantry, you probably did

Why do I say all of this? America's court systems have, for

some time now, been weighted against fathers when it comes to child custody. Although there are exceptions, in most cases, the mother will gain custody of the children while the father will be expected to pay for them. While I have no sympathy for deadbeat dads, I do believe there are a lot of good fathers who get screwed over in divorce court. You have to be proactive if you want to avoid this fate.

While I'm generally against divorce, I know there are sometimes good reasons. I do advocate that you suck it up and stay in an unhappy marriage while kids are little (under ten?). I do not advise staying in a marriage where you are being abused, or you and the children are in danger from your spouse. You will have to make your own decisions on infidelity. The truth is that it happens more than people admit, but many couples do learn to get past it.

Both of you need to communicate and make the after-marriage work. Think of all the new extended families who actually take turns raising the kids. I know plenty of married couples who are secretly jealous of their divorced friends for this reason. And the kids? Hey, what kid doesn't want multiple Christmases? Just remember that even if you're pissed at each other, it's your kids who take it the hardest. Be responsible and act like adults. At least while they're in the room.

Not all couples who divorce go to war in court. Some realize that hiring lawyers only makes lawyers richer, and they learn to divide up their stuff reasonably. If you're being fair, you can agree to 50/50 custody on kids. Then start valuing everything in the home and decide who gets what, with consideration to value.

I'm hoping that, if you're divorcing, your kids are a little older. Maybe in their teens. You should talk to them about where they would like to live. They may want to stay in their current school, but not always if one of you is moving somewhere better.

And by the way. If you have kids and you're still so shallow and rotten that you rush out to get restraining orders, sabotage your ex at every turn, and try to fuck them over both as a parent and financially, then not only shame on you but, you guessed it, go fuck yourself!

INFANTS AND TODDLERS
RED PHASE

It was a nice sunny day, and forty-eight brand new privates fresh out of reception were enjoying a leisurely bus ride to their first day of basic training. I think their bus driver even played some music for them, and some of them had drifted off to sleep as the bus pulled to a stop. Suddenly, like babies who've left the warmth of the womb for a cold hospital room and a smack on the ass from a creepy old doctor, forty-eight privates were descended on by nearly a dozen angry drill sergeants. They were yelling and screaming, looking for any signs of weakness or worse, defiance. The shark attack was on. Duffle bags were everywhere, and one Private Snuffy had dropped his paperwork. "That's OK Private," a nice drill sergeant told him, "sometimes you just gotta crawl before you can walk. All the way into the barracks Private, LOW CRAWL!!!"

OK, SO WE'VE GONE OVER ALL THE PRE-CHILD questions and how to pick a good battle buddy. At this point, I assume you already know how babies are made, and you didn't need a chapter for that. If you do, Private Snuffy has been leaving some great artwork in the latrine stalls that should be educational for you. Since this is a "self-help" book and not the *Penthouse* letters forum, let's just skip to the actual babies.

When you have your first baby, it's pretty damn intense. They're fragile, completely dependent, and you're lucky if they let you sleep two hours a damn night. You spend the first few months with bags under your eyes and baby puke on your shirt, and the little fart hasn't even started crawling yet.

This is the period in their life when you'll have to spend the most time taking care of them. Think of it like Red Phase in basic training, when your drill sergeant was always there watching every last thing you did. Babies, like privates, can't really do anything for themselves besides poop and cry a lot, so you're just going to have to suck it up and give them the extra attention.

Ladies, I know you won't believe this, but your babies will be fine if you need to take a break. Try to set a regular routine for eating and sleeping, and stick to it. Once you have them trained, you'll be better able to plan some relaxation or get things done around the house.

Fellas, pull up your man britches and start doing your part. Learn to change a diaper and cook (just don't use the same finger to taste the soup that you just tested the diaper with, you sick bastard). Spend some time with your child when you get home from work. Yes, I'm assuming you're in a traditional household where dad works and mom raises the baby. After the infant/toddler years, you may want to switch the roles up, but early on trust me when I say moms are better at this.

If you thought the infant stage was tough, you're wrong. They become toddlers and reach the age of two. This is when you are most likely to just fucking kill yourself. This is the part where you will look over at your spouse at 0200 hours, both of you covered in baby puke or shit, and Rochambeau over who will get up and deal with the crying baby this time. Gentlemen, you will likely always lose, because she has the vagina.

The Drill Sergeant's Guide to Parenting

. . .

Nature vs. Nurture

IF YOU WENT to any level of college or watched enough daytime therapy television, you've probably heard of the debate between nature and nurture. Nature refers to what we are biologically predisposed to do, while nurture suggests that we can train certain behaviors out of children. You might think because I'm a Drill Sergeant that I lean to the nature side of things (nurture is a sissy word. I prefer the word *coerce*). However, you'd then be forgetting that in the Army we strive to train the stupidity out of young privates all the time.

The military is not a natural environment though. Unless you are monitoring and controlling your kids' behavior every second, which I really don't recommend, their nature will come out. You can take away the toy laser gun and give your son a Barbie dream car, but as soon as you're not looking, he'll be making finger guns and blowing that shit up in an imaginary explosion of epic fucking proportions.

I've found it best to let your kids be themselves. My middle child, upon seeing me take her older sister hunting, really wanted to spend some time with me. She asked if I would take her fishing. Being a dad who likes a little fishing, I happily agreed. When Saturday morning rolled around though, I practically spit out my coffee as she came out in a nice yellow dress. I informed my little princess that she would probably want to wear jeans for this mission. Then she looked at me with those angelic little eyes and said, "Do you think we could just go for a nice breakfast somewhere?" Well, holy shit, what could I do? Of course, I said yes! And to top it all off, we found a shared love of bacon that transcends all debates of how to raise your kids. Always, always, always enjoy your time with them whenever you can. You'll thank me later.

Liberty vs. Security

WHILE WE'RE on the subject of authoritarian parenting, I want to introduce a new concept to you. I believe most political/social conflicts can be boiled down to the balance between liberty and security. When the government taxes you, it is taking some of your economic liberty. If they use the money to provide a police force, then they are providing you with security. The more security they provide the people, the more liberty they are usually taking in the process.

The authority and discipline you provide your little booger eaters is similar to this. Think about it. We do not give ten-year old's the liberty of gambling at the casino. We do not give toddlers the liberty of hanging out by the freeway with no supervision. To do so would deprive them of the safety and security they need.

Children need a certain amount of security (rules, boundaries) to feel safe in this world. While liberty can spark creativity, too much is dangerous. While I chose to give my children a high level of security, I can't make this choice for you in all areas. You will need to decide, based on your kid's maturity level and intelligence, how much liberty they can handle. I encourage you as much as possible, to look at parenting issues as a balance of liberty and security. It may help you with some tough decisions.

* * *

Do's and Don'ts

OK LISTEN UP. I'm sure by now all of you have watched a YouTube video showing people doing really stupid things like swinging from a rope but not making it to the water or landing a four-wheeler on their stinking head. These are the same types of people you see at the county fair who make you feel better about yourself but cause you to fear for the future of our nation. I'm listing some Do's and Don'ts here of baby raising so that you don't become like one of the stupid people I just mentioned.

Do hold your baby to comfort and calm them. Do give them a warm bath in a small tub. Do dry them off with a nice soft towel afterward. Do NOT give them alcohol to help them relax (no matter what your alcoholic Grandma says). Do not wash them with a garden hose, and do not put them in the dryer afterward (no ladies, not even a hair dryer).

DO NOT EVER leave a baby in the car. I shouldn't have to say this, but it happens. You will become tired and distracted during this phase. If you are a former soldier treat that baby like you would your weapon. Dummy cord it to your freaking neck if you have too, but do not forget your baby and leave them to the elements. Babies are a lot like 2nd Lieutenants, and leaving them in the car can and will kill them. Use your head soldier!

Do let them play with crayons (for some of you numskulls this will apply to your kids all the way into adulthood), but do not let them play with permanent markers. In fact, why the hell do you even have those in your house? Do let your kids pretend to be firemen with the hose out back. Do not own garden hoses that can reach inside your house (my son actually did this). Do feed your babies that ground up apple stuff with the baby picture on the front. Do not, for the love of God, give your baby chili. And yes, for my Mexican friends out there reading this, I understand you were raised with hot sauce in your baby bottles, and you think none of this applies to you. Fuck you Poncho Villa, your baby's shit stinks too.

Do not leave out tools and electric appliances for them to discover. At one point, I made the mistake (yes, I do make them sometimes) of leaving out a hot iron on the ironing board. I believe I was letting it cool off, and my then three-year-old son was preoccupied with his toys, or so I thought. Fortunately, no one was hurt, and the house wasn't burnt down. However, for several months our living room carpet had a hole in it shaped like an iron.

Toilet Training

Yup. Here's the unglamorous side of parenting. I wish I could tell you that parents in this country fought the good fight and that no Drill Sergeant ever had to tell army privates how to use the damn latrine. I wish I could tell you that, but the army is no fairy tale, and neither is parenting. Sigh.

Experts will tell you that most kids really can't be toilet trained until they're around two. Obviously, there are going to be exceptions on either side of that. Usually, the parents who train their kids earlier than two are maintaining a constant vigil and watching for the signs that the kid is about to crap their pants, then running them to the toilet. The point is though, that toilet training your kid is more about the effort you put into it than what comes out of them. Children become more self-aware around two and begin to realize that a messy diaper is both uncomfortable and embarrassing.

Boys and girls are also different when it comes to toilet training. As my female readers already know, girls tend to advance faster than boys and can be toilet trained a little younger. Some of you ladies may like to believe this is evidence of your superiority. However, I have obtained some good intel suggesting this phenomenon is simply because boys could fucking care less about their soggy diaper; they have more important shit to do. They swing back to this attitude as they become old men sometimes.

As with everything else with kids, toilet training has several equipment options (honestly, children seem to have more gear than soldiers do). There's the miniature toilet seats with the little plastic bedpans under them, for those of you who want some extra cleaning. Or there are seat adapters so you can put them on the real toilet. Note to Private Snuffy, do not just sit your eighteen-month-old on a full-sized toilet seat and think they won't fall through, Numnuts! I also highly recommend you invest in a lot of disposable wet wipes (yes, the same ones you use out in the field, Snuffy).

I must say there is also a psychological side to proper toilet training. Kids left to neglect will often not come around as quickly as those who are cared for. When my youngest child was of this age, my wife was working, and we had him in daycare. They were good folks, but there were multiple kids there for them to keep track of. At the age of two he still was not toilet trained, and at one point he decided to grace our wall with some fecal artwork! After some serious discussion, my wife made the decision to stop working and spend more time with him. It meant financial cutbacks for us, but the behavior changes in our son were almost immediate. There is truly no substitute for a loving parent.

The bottom line in toilet training is that you will have to be vigilant, and actually put time into your child if you want them properly toilet trained. You're also going to have to help with butt wiping, and that's just gross. Have fun troops!

. . .

Spanking

I GREW up in a world where spanking existed. Hell, spanking was mild then compared to the other shit. We still had the belt. Or the spoon. Or mom's hairbrush. This was all before politically correct liberal therapists took over and decided it was better to let our children become angry, self-absorbed brats that shoot up their schools when they don't get their way.

I'm actually not an advocate of BEATING your child, but spankings work. And after one session with the belt, trust me on this, they will learn to respect and fear the sound of your belt clearing the loops on your pants. They will suddenly stop setting each other on fire and clean up their damn mess.

The best way to know you're not overdoing it is to follow a simple rule. Try not to spank them in anger. I say try because the little shits will seriously piss you off. However, take a deep breath. Remain calm. Slowly pull out your belt, and proceed to wage war on their bratty little backsides. It's like therapy for both of you!

If you're a busybody liberal who sees me spanking my kids in public and you feel the need to get in my business, be prepared for a big heaping of go fuck yourself.

THEY LEARN From You

THEY'RE WATCHING YOU. Like little inmates, they are watching, and listening, and learning from everything you do. They see where the cereal is kept, and they will figure out how to climb on the counter. They notice child safety locks and how you open them. And they will repeat your most embarrassing phrases.

I remember one fine weekend morning when our kids were very little. I was enjoying my coffee, and DS Mom went out to check on her gardening in the backyard. She had just recently planted some rose bushes, as I recall. Then the little ones and I were shocked by loud screaming out back. We rushed to the back porch to see what was the matter.

There was my lovely wife, in her Saturday morning Walmart attire, chasing our beloved family dog around the backyard with a shovel. The new rose bushes were overturned. The fresh dirt was dug up. And my wife had murder in her eyes. We watched for a few moments until she let out a rather *unladylike* phrase.

"You FUCKING dog!"

Of course, this was understandable and I was going to let it pass with just a chuckle. But then, our beloved two-year-old daughter, my little princess no less, repeated this wonderful phrase.

"Yeah, you FUCKING dog!"

Our older child, even my wife, and I all stood speechless for a moment. The dog saw his opportunity and slinked away to hide. The rest of us just looked at our sweet, angelic little child who had just dropped a perfect F-bomb. I was getting ready to make a wisecrack, but my oldest daughter, then about five, beat me to it.

"Nice going Mom!" she said.

I just shook my head. In retrospect, though, it is still a story we love retelling at our family table. Shit, maybe I am a bad parent!

Maintaining Your Maleness and Womanhood

Men, I realize that minivans have a certain convenience to them when you have multiple children. But if you're driving a minivan while she's in a sporty sedan, you've lost your man card. No, you don't have to make it worse with a pink polo. Just because her friends say out loud that you're a great guy doesn't mean any of them would ever have sex with you (they're her friends they're *supposed* to despise you). And no, a hipster beard and skinny jeans do not make you look any manlier.

What does make you manlier is the BBQ. It is in your DNA and your heritage to own and master the grill. This is where you earn back the respect of your fellow men as you sit out back in the summer heat and chug beers where she is less likely to come out and catch you. If she does, just pour some on the flames and tell her it's a safety tool. If you grew up in a *progressive* household and the grill intimidates you, start with something easy like wieners (even you should know your way around those, freak). Get some practice before you start burning the crap out of T-bones and porterhouses.

Women, being a mom does not mean you have to give up all appearance of looking like a woman. You don't have to cut your hair off like a Siberian prisoner and wear burlap jumpsuits just to prove to everyone that you no longer give a shit what you look like. Think of how jealous you will make your friends when you show up with your babies in a designer stroller and still have silky long hair past your shoulders. Good luck getting baby shit out of your hair though.

The costs

Let me say to both of you that when you have infants, it's also likely the period of your life when you're starting out and don't make a lot of money. Babies are said to cost families upwards of $10,000 a year. There's formula, diapers, strollers, cribs, and so much more. It can be very stressful, and money issues separate a lot of young couples. This doesn't have to be you.

Talk to each other about your budget. Be up front regarding costs and expenses. Don't go out splurging on useless crap like a new set of golf clubs or fancy heels when you can't afford it. It's really easy to go on spending sprees and then not tell your partner, but trust me when I say that is a breach of trust in your relationship that nearly equals infidelity.

I can't tell you how many times my wife and I had to cut costs when we were starting out. In harder times, cable TV was usually the first thing to go. Then you look at phone bills, non-necessity foods, even the beer and wine gets cut (yikes). One of you may have to take an extra job and get less sleep. Just remember, in these hard times that many people before you have done this and they made it. You will make it too. Suck it up and make it happen.

If you are a single mom (remember how I advised against this?), it can be even harder. Putting your child in day care pretty much eats up whatever you make at work, but you should know that there are a lot of services out there to help someone in your situation. Forget my disparaging remarks about welfare, swallow your pride, and go get some help. Every county in America has social services. Your baby comes first, and that means doing what you have to do to provide the basic necessities.

Dads, if you're reading this and you're not helping support your children, you are what we in civilized America call a DEADBEAT. Stop being a scumbag and support your offspring! If you are a single dad and you are raising your children, the same services and support are there for you. If Private Snuffy is reading this right now, regardless of your situation, go beat your face. Do pushups until I get tired. Because I said so. Then go fuck yourself.

. . .

Marital Relations

Keeping the flame alive could be a problem for some of you in this stage. For others it takes longer, hence the *seven-year itch*, but a lot of relationships experience it at about four years. If you have a couple of little ones, or even just one, you might be reaching this point. Relations between you and your battle buddy could be stressed by the behavior of your children at this point. It could also be that *relations* between you and your partner are non-existent.

The first thing to understand is you're not alone. Lots of parents go through this. Your grandparents may have had separate beds for this reason. Mom (or the selected homemaker) is at home all day while dad is working. She's tired. She's a little stir crazy from only having babies to talk too. She's not really worried about wearing nice clothes or even daily showers. Running a house is time-consuming, and she's not feeling romantic when dad walks in the door.

Dad (or the breadwinner) has it a little differently. He works hard at his job which tends to have defined hours. When those hours are done, he wants to come home and relax. He may be stressed from a boss or First Sergeant who is an asshole, and there's nothing better for stress than romantic relations at home. But mom isn't having it. She's ready to hand him the kids and run screaming out the door. When dad tries to get frisky, she looks at him like he's crazy. Now, he feels rejected, and she feels that he only values her for something other than her brilliant mind. Ladies, we truly do value you for more than your body, believe me. However, food and sex are pretty high priorities for most men, and if you didn't already know this, you haven't been paying attention.

These stressors can be just as hard on the relationship as money issues. If you do not communicate with each other, you may find yourself unloading on your friends. Good friends will listen and console you, but it doesn't fix the problem. Bad friends will steer you away from solving the problem and may even poison your relationship. Either way, the one person you need to communicate with here is your partner. Talk to your battle buddy, and work it out. Most of the time, you'll find that just talking about it will alleviate the problems. Not as much as getting drunk and rolling each other in the hay, but it helps.

Advice From Others

At some point in your parenthood, usually when your kids are very young, you will get a lot of unsolicited advice. More often than not, those giving the advice are doing so for their own sense of superiority rather than to actually give you any fucking help. There's an air of pretension when one is able to point out other people's failures. Even more so when they can tell you how you're doing it wrong.

I used to get this in basic training sometimes; sometimes from some jerkwad drill sergeant in another battalion, but (even more annoyingly) from non-drill sergeants. God help them if it was some punk Corporal. "Hey Drill Sergeant," they'd say, "your troops look like shit. Maybe you should work on that."

Yeah. How 'bout you GO FUCK YOURSELF!

It's even more annoying as a parent. You'll hear it from other parents, how unruly your children are. You should spank them. You shouldn't spank them. You shouldn't raise your voice. You need to be more firm. The worst was always those who didn't have kids of their own but considered themselves an expert (like those in the education system). Even if they don't say it, you can see them thinking to themselves how they'll do it better. When I see that look, I just laugh. Everyone has a plan till they get punched in the face. Or in this case, everyone thinks they're a tough parent until your soggy-diapered booger-eating two-year-old throws a full-blown screaming fit over some Lucky Charms in the fucking grocery store.

I'm not saying you won't have to be strong sometimes and resist what they want. I'm just telling you that, every now and then, you will decide which hill to die on and maybe just get them the fucking Happy Meal with the shitty toy. You will let them go outside with no jacket or looking like they escaped the loony bin because you're too exhausted to fight them over it anymore. Just remember to take pictures and embarrass the shit out of them when they are teenagers. It may be your only satisfaction, but definitely worth it.

CHILDREN AGES FOUR THROUGH TWELVE
WHITE PHASE

So, there we were, up before the crack of dawn getting ready for a field exercise, and one of the goofy little twits had forgotten his rain poncho. His squad leader was supposed to have checked everyone's gear, but instead, he tries to save the situation by telling his Drill Sergeant that it was OK because it wasn't supposed to rain that day. My battle gets this evil look in his eye and tells the privates "Drill Sergeants can make it rain."
One garden hose and forty-eight soaked Private Snuffies later, they started to understand.

OK PARENTS, BY NOW YOU'RE A BIT MORE SEASONED at raising kids. You may have more than one child now and you're on your way to completing your family. Mom is no longer nervous with babies and carries them like a football while she cooks dinner and talks on the phone at the same time. Dad is now fully converted to pastel polo shirts and parallel parking the minivan. He can BBQ a mean chicken too. Just don't get him started on his mother in law after two or three cocktails.

As a veteran father, I can tell you that the years of four

through twelve are my favorite with the kids. This is a time of learning and exploration. It's a time of bicycles and baseballs, tree houses and sleepovers, and swim suits and scraped knees. If I could go back in time to any age, I'd be eight years old on summer vacation. Does it get any better?

This is also the critical time to start teaching your children values. I say this because it's really hard to teach your two-year-old morals, and if you wait until they're teenagers, you'll probably be picking them up from the police station a lot. What values should you teach them? I realize this could be a tough question for today's modern parent, especially if you attended public schools.

A few years ago, the US Army was going through this dilemma. We were teaching young soldiers how to shoot and read maps, but we hadn't focused on a clear value system. Many of them came from less than functional homes and didn't have strong morals either. The results were disastrous. Soldier on soldier crimes were rising, including soldiers committing major crimes while off duty. It was a situation that needed to be addressed.

Enter the Army Values. Seven words for soldiers to live by. Loyalty, Duty, Respect, Selfless Service, Honor, Integrity, and Personal Courage. If your kids aren't already in church or Boy Scouts by now, you may want to consider these words yourself. Let's go over the seven values now.

Loyalty

Bear true faith and allegiance to the US constitution, the Army, and other soldiers. Be loyal to the nation and its heritage.

The Drill Sergeant's Guide to Parenting

YOUR CHILDREN SHOULD BE loyal to you, your spouse, and each other. Sometimes it comes naturally, but it often has to be taught. Reward them when they follow the instructions you lay out for them, and make sure to discipline them when they don't. If you do this at home, you won't end up like one of those moms crawling through the ball pit at the pizza funhouse trying to catch your little brat in front of smirking bystanders. If you do end up like those moms, let me just advise you that spankings are best delivered back at the car or at home where there are no witnesses.

Loyalty is the first value you should teach your children. It's a value that is really lacking in American society now, with the exception of sports fans. For some reason, millions of Americans have traded their loyalty to their country and fellow citizens for loyalty to overpaid athletes.

Duty

Fulfill your obligations. Accept responsibility for your own actions and those entrusted to your care. Find opportunities to improve oneself for the good of the group.

AS A PARENT OF MULTIPLE CHILDREN, there's nothing more frustrating than leaving them with a list of chores, only to come home from work and find that nothing has been done. It wasn't even a big list! Instead, they're on the couch surrounded by candy wrappers, a popcorn bowl, and empty soda cans! Although I try very hard not to take the Army home with me, this situation tends to bring out my Drill Sergeant voice. "The chore list just tripled dirtbags."

Instilling a sense of duty in your children is not easy. It takes constant attention, but it's important. Better to teach them now than to see them get fired from their first job. It's just going to reflect on you anyways.

Accepting responsibility for their actions is the other side of this coin. When you have one kid it's always obvious who made the mess, but when there's three it becomes a mystery. Now we have to interrogate, ahem, question them. They eventually get really good at playing innocent or throwing their siblings under the bus. This is where you have to use some Drill Sergeant tactics. When you can't get to the bottom of the mystery, just punish all of them equally until someone fesses up. This helps teach them about teamwork, or at least prompts the innocent parties to smack the guilty one once you've left the room.

Respect

Rely upon the golden rule. How we consider others reflects upon each of us, both personally and as a professional organization.

TREATING others as they should be treated is another important value for your kids. No one likes bullies, but for some reason when you get a group of kids together, the bullies come out and run the show. For some other strange reason, giving bullies the whole "how would you like it" spiel never seems to work. If you catch your kids bullying others, you should discipline the shit out of them. Then maybe seek counseling, because somewhere along the line you screwed things up.

Now, if your child is not a bully, they will at some point end up on the receiving end of bullying. This is frustrating for a parent and will cause you to fantasize laying some serious smack down on the little ingrate's parents like Colin Farrel in *True Detective*. There's a learning opportunity for your child as you teach them to hand out their smack down. OK, I know, first we have to tell them to try and handle it in a civil manner with their words. This is what your child's teachers will insist on, so go ahead and let them use this method (again for learning purposes).

Once they have done this, and, as expected, the bully has not only laughed at them but carried out further aggressions, tell your child to stand up for themselves. Trust me, this isn't easy, but it works. Once your little hero has punched the offender in the nose a couple times, the offending child will usually back off and harass someone else's kid. Please note that in today's liberal public schools your child will likely get in trouble, but they will have gained self-respect at having dished out some real American justice. When they grow up, they will be better at standing up for themselves and not get walked on by all the workplace bullies they'll encounter. They may also go the extra step and protect someone else's child from bullies (now that's Army material!).

SELFLESS SERVICE

Put the welfare of the nation, the army, and your subordinates before your own.

THINK about the Boy Scouts for a moment (yes, I know, Girl Scouts do good deeds too, but they also sell highly addictive snacks and take people's money). They get merit badges for mowing lawns or helping old ladies cross the street. Think of how much better our society would be if more kids were offering their help to others in need. Taking it a step further, we want to encourage kids to do the right thing even when there is no reward or merit badge. That is selfless service!

Like any other value, this is hard to instill in kids. Especially with all the distractions out there. Why stop to help the old lady when your favorite Pokemon character is right around the corner? Like any other value, this is one kids learn best from their parents. When was the last time you helped someone else with no thought of reward? Your miniature Private Snuffies are watching you. Lead by example!

Think of some ways your youngsters can be a help around your home and neighborhood. Does your neighbor's lawn need mowing? Maybe they're out of town and need someone to feed their pets? Involving your children in your community will teach them selfless service and make them better citizens. It also puts them in a good position to spot secret terrorist activities and report them back to you and the proper authorities. Then the nice agents from the FBI can stop by and fuck their shit up. Your kids might even get a medal! Happy Faces all around! Drill Sergeant can dream, can't he?

Honor

Live up to all the Army values.

I KNOW what you're thinking. Honor sounds really repetitive to the other values. Even the bureaucrats who wrote the description couldn't come up with something better than "live up to the other values," but honor is an important value for your kids to learn. It's becoming a rarity in our country, and it's up to parents like you to start bringing it back.

But what is honor? Is it simply opening doors for the ladies? No, that's just chivalry. How about obeying the law? Close, but not all laws are moral and immoral people might simply behave to avoid punishment. If Private Snuffy is following the basic rules I lay out, but lets his fellow soldier get into trouble when he could have spoken up, he's going to get his ass chewed as well.

Honor is a bit like integrity. If the best meaning of integrity is to *do what's right when no one is looking,* then honor would be more like doing what's right even if it's going to cost you. When your kid stands up for another kid who is being bullied, that's the honorable thing to do. When a young man realizes that a young woman is too intoxicated to be giving consent and helps her into the front seat of the car rather than the back seat, that is the honorable thing to do.

Look, anyone can follow the rules when they're scared of the consequences or expect a reward. Raise your kids to be honorable, even when it means a few rules (and maybe someone's nose) get broken. This is one of those values your child's public-school teachers will probably try to *culture* out of them. Teachers like that can go fuck themselves. Teach your kids to grow a spine and make your grandparents proud.

* * *

Integrity

Do what is right, legally and morally. Be willing to do what is right even when no one is looking.

THERE WAS a time in my youth when I was a snot-nosed, grabasstic, know it all. Yes, even your Drill Sergeant was once a teenager. I was getting myself into trouble and my father had to read me the riot act. In one of these sessions, he told me he had no respect for liars and thieves. It sat with me pretty good, and to this day I don't steal things (in the Army we call it "appropriating." Just kidding). I also try not to lie to people (OK you get an excuse for fishing or hunting stories. That's not lying it's exaggerating).

I think integrity is really nicely summed up by the kid who finds the wallet and promptly turns it in. Maybe they get a reward, maybe they don't. The point is they did the right thing. You should try to instill in your children a sense of integrity. Cookies make great bait for this. No kid can resist a nice cookie. Leave one out with a note saying, "don't eat." Just don't do this when dad is home. If he's anything like Private Snuffy, he'll let the brat take the heat for his sugar stealing and instead of learning integrity your little monster will just need therapy.

Honesty kind of falls under integrity. Often though, we focus on teaching kids to be honest to us and to others but not always with themselves. Honesty with yourself is different. Our society tends to gloss stuff over and tell ourselves everything's fine when it really isn't. Asking yourself if you really need those expensive shoes, gadget, or second helping of ice cream can be harder than fessing up for something you did wrong. You should teach your kids to be honest with themselves as well as others. It will help them establish a greater personal integrity.

PERSONAL COURAGE

Face fear, danger, or adversity. Both physical and moral courage.

MOST OF YOU reading this know what courage is. For some, it means overcoming your fears. For others, it can mean facing real danger. In my view, there are two different kinds of courage, and it's up to us to master both of them. Teaching your children both physical and moral courage is another important value our society needs more of.

Let's talk physical courage first. In the Army, I demanded that hundreds of Private Snuffies face their fear of danger. Sometimes they faced it on rope bridges (fear of heights), sometimes with heavy weapons, and sometimes with just plain ole fear of their angry ass drill sergeant. I can tell you that, with a few exceptions, most trainees face their fears and make it through boot camp. Some go on to face even greater dangers in real combat zones. Military service members are some of the bravest people on the freaking planet.

It can be really easy as parents to overprotect our children from modern dangers. From bicycle helmets to keeping them locked inside, we tend to let our worries overrule their sense of adventure. Get your kid a bike and off of their PlayStation. Take them hiking, or fishing, or even riding dirt bikes and four-wheelers. For crying out loud, let your kid get dirty! Give them a pocket knife and some band-aids, and send them out into the woods! When they turn thirty, you do not want them calling you every time they fearfully try to leave your basement.

Moral courage is also something that needs to be taught. Mark Twain once said, "It is curious that physical courage should be so common in the world and moral courage so rare." Think about it. You probably know a lot of people who would run into a burning building to save a life, but how many people do you know who are brave enough to stand up at city hall and complain about the latest ordinance?

Moral courage is harder to find because physical pain is often not as scary as the mental pain. Private Snuffy crawls through the mud and sand because he fears my wrath. I know a lot of big, tough guys who would rather wade into a firefight than give a public speech. It's the fear of non-acceptance that dissuades us. Yet, your freedom of speech is the number one most important right that so many in the military gave their lives to preserve. A lot of adults in this country need to get over their fear of non-acceptance and start speaking up.

Teaching your children courage doesn't just mean swinging from a frayed rope over a dark pit full of poisonous snakes (although that is really good fun). It means teaching them to stand up for themselves and the rights of their fellow citizens. Remember that freedom is only a generation away from being lost forever, and if America goes under so does the rest of the world. Your children are the world's next guardians of freedom and hope. But not Private Snuffy's children. Those little window lickers couldn't guard a free case of syphilis.

Back Sassing

AT SOME POINT in this stage, they are going to start back talking you. This is where they start to assert themselves, test boundaries, and learn their place in this world. So, don't be alarmed, it's perfectly natural for them to do this. Boundaries are like borders; however, without them we have neither inner family discipline or a damn country. So, it's your job to enforce the rules here.

There's really a lot of ways to deal with this problem. Some parents dish out spankings. Others threaten to take away stuff. I know of others who force-feed soap or even apple cider vinegar (yuck). Obviously, their age matters. When a two-year-old asserts themselves, you do need to put a stop to it, even if it's cute and you're trying not to laugh. When your teenager does it, it's more likely to invoke your anger and have you reaching for the baseball bat.

Always use common sense and adjust your level of discipline to what your child needs. Some kids are good with soap in the mouth or to have their cell phone taken away. Others just need a damn ass whooping. The bottom line is that you cannot let them walk all over you. Allowing unacceptable behavior at young ages creates even more unacceptable behavior when they get older. It ends with you being miserable and making a lot of excuses for why your worthless brat is in prison.

GUNS. The West Wasn't Won on Salad.

I GREW up in a family that hunted and owned guns. We were in a small town surrounded by a lot of people like us, so the thought that there were people out there who didn't teach their kids to properly use firearms seemed strange to us. As a Drill Sergeant, I've seen more and more kids come through the Army who actually have never fired a weapon before in their life. Sometimes that makes the job of teaching them easier as they haven't learned any bad habits, but it does concern me.

If you have firearms in your home and you have children, you need to make them aware of the firearms and teach them proper safety. There's nothing more dangerous than a curious kid who just found daddy's handgun and has no idea it can really go off. All of my kids know that guns are dangerous because I've personally trained them on a range. I take them hunting so they can see just how powerful our weapons are (it also stocks the freezer quite nicely, thank you).

Kids who are raised by responsible adults with firearms grow up to become responsible adults with firearms. If you are not teaching them proper firearm safety, trust me when I say they are learning the wrong techniques somewhere else. When Hollywood actors are not on the news telling us guns are bad, they are making millions promoting gun violence in movies. Boys are especially susceptible to this and need your guidance.

Guns are not always the answer. I was raised with firearms and then later received training from the US Military. If you are not confident with firearms but already own them, you need to seek out some proper training. A lot of firing ranges can refer you to instructors that can go over the basics with you. Often the instructors are former military or law enforcement, and they just want to help make you a safer citizen. And for heaven's sake, don't become one of those pansy anti-gun whackos. Those of us who own responsibly take our freedom seriously and don't need you trying to infringe it. Go to Canada hippy.

* * *

Religion

AT BASIC TRAINING, we used to get a lot of new religious converts every Sunday. Going to church was a way to get out of barracks duties and, on some bases, a way for Private Snuffy to sneak a peek at actual female soldiers who were in attendance. I always figured that, even if they went for the wrong reasons, some of the good stuff might actually get through their thick skulls and make them better people. It's not what brought you, it's the fact that you came, right?

Like a lot of Americans, I've had mixed feelings about religion. Our nation was founded on Judeo-Christian values. It's a huge part of what makes us so great, and also why others from less tolerant religions and cultures hate us. I don't always find myself in church, but I believe in God, and that he has a purpose for me. There are countless times that I prayed for help in my life and received not only comfort but the help I needed.

Whether you attend every Sunday or just reflect on your own, it's a conversation you need to have with your kids. Whatever your ancestry or heritage, you're an American. Your kids are American. They need to know about the values that helped make our country a shining light for everyone else in this world. They need to know the values that so many in our military have fought and died for. It wasn't just for freedom of speech and to own a firearm. It was so that you could worship without fear of retaliation from those in our government.

Sadly, rights that are not exercised run the risk of being lost. And your kids likely won't participate in church if you don't encourage them. Faith can help them grow, and can be an amazing co-parent if you help guide them. Get them involved in a Bible study or a religious youth group of some sort and then talk to them about it. Yes, they will make their own decisions someday, but you can help guide them and be the one they turn to when they have questions. Unless they ask stupid questions like Private Snuffy. Then they get pushups.

Camping

THE OUTDOORS IS a great way to bond with your kids, and I do recommend that you take them hunting, fishing, and camping. It's fun for them and makes for good memories. It also means when they grow up and join the army, I won't have to see those stupid looks on their faces the first time they sleep in the woods!

There's probably nothing more American than loading up the kids and gear and driving up to the lake every summer. The outdoors includes campfires, dirt, marshmallows, more dirt, mosquitoes, no internet signal, bugs, dirt, hot dogs, wild animals, and dirt. It's freaking amazing!

Camping takes a little work on your part. You have to get off your butt and load the vehicle. You have the drag the kids, sometimes screaming, from their electronic zombification devices. You have to arrange for the pets to be fed or take them with you. If you're like me you will drive too fast up the winding roads, and everyone will get car sick, but every last bit of effort is worth it when you are there on the lake, watching your kids actually come alive and enjoy the outdoors a while. Take their cell phones away for a while, it won't kill them. Just keep yours handy as you'll want the pictures. These are the memories your kids will cherish for years to come.

* * *

Money

DURING THIS PHASE of their lives, it's a great time to start teaching them about money. Not just how to count it or how much it buys at the store, but how to earn it. There's probably no better way to teach them about the rewards of work than with a good lawn mowing or babysitting job. Here they will also learn about responsibility and keeping their promises. However, if you are in some totalitarian liberal state like California, I don't advise letting your kids open a lemonade stand.

You could give your kid an allowance, or like some parents, you could just give them money when they ask for it. Maybe you had a good night at the casino and feel guilty about ditching them with their cranky aunt for a night, so you just throw them some Benjamins and hope they don't hate you later? Not a great idea.

I believe you should always make money a reward for having done something like dishes or laundry. Granted, there are some chores they should do just for getting to live in your house, but if you want them to learn about money you could occasionally pay them.

Once they have money, you'll want to teach them about how to spend it wisely. Teach them to save up for the things they really want, like bicycles, dollhouses, and stock options. Better yet, show them how to invest their money in something that helps them make more. Just not some lame pyramid scheme. Please, for the love of God, no.

* * *

Fitness

This is also the time to start thinking about their fitness. I really didn't train my kids too hard at this age. I wanted them to just enjoy being kids. However, my kids inherited my metabolism and didn't have weight problems either.

In recent years, the US Army has noticed that our country's youth are becoming more and more overweight. This makes whipping them into fighting shape when they join the military even harder. As parents and fellow members of our great nation, you have some responsibility here.

Now again, I don't recommend a full weight-lifting regimen for eight-year-olds. I do recommend keeping an eye on your child's weight! If they have love handles and man boobs before the age of ten, you've got a problem there. Chances are also good they learned their eating habits from you. So, get them off the couch and take them to the gym with you. I suggest the tread mill lard butt!

OK, not everyone can afford the gym. No problem. I recommend a workout routine that you can do two or three days a week. Maybe just forty-five minutes. Pushups, crunches, jumping jacks, lunges, planks, air squats. Mix it up and go for a jog every now and then. This is stuff your kids can do with you when you're ready.

While I did not have a problem with my girls, when my son came along I found it harder to keep him in shape. They were always on the go and had a love for volleyball. He, however, developed a love for video games. If you're a parent of boys, you probably have experienced this. It became very easy to throw the kid some pizza and a video game, and let him hide out in his room for days at a time. It might make your job easier, but it's not good parenting and not best for him.

On the flip side, I found that allowing him an agreed upon

amount of time on the game system worked to get chores and exercise from him. Each day, he first had to do whatever chores were his to do, then an outside physical activity of some sort. In the summer, this usually meant swimming. Once he accomplished those, he could have some game time. I found this system worked really well, and often he would get caught up in the outside activities for longer than we expected. Why? Because he was having fun, and by the time he was done, occasionally I would be home in time to play some video games with him. Nothing quite bonds a father and son like blowing stuff up and killing bad guys on TV!

About Those Video Games

I realize not everyone thinks video games are great for kids. To an extent, I do agree. When you can, you should turn off the electronics and take your kids outside somewhere. Obviously, that might not always be the option you're going to take. In recent years, the incidents of kids going crazy and shooting people has also become a problem. Violent video games are one of the things we point to as a possible reason.

I'm one of those people who grew up watching Bugs Bunny get chased by a shotgun-wielding Elmer Fudd. I also played Cowboys and Indians or Cops and Robbers with the other kids. As long as boys are boys, violence will always be a part of their creative play. I have a hard time blaming video games. Especially when I look at our society and the number of kids who are growing up without a positive male role model in their homes.

When my son and I play a military style game that involves shooting enemies, I do understand the concern. I explain to my son, much like when we watch action movies, that this isn't real and we are just killing bad guys for fun. In the real world, we don't always get to the kill the bad guys. Instead, the bad guys go to jail for a few months and then get released and find some welfare mom to live off of while they look for their next victim. Which always begs the question: Why don't we shoot bad guys anymore? And why do women on welfare like felons so much? I'm sure neither answer is that my son and I play too many video games.

The point is, real life sucks sometimes. It's OK to take a break from it and get caught up in a fantasy world, but only after your chores are done. Boys aren't the only ones with weird, violent fantasies. Have you read some of the teen-vampire sex books your girls are reading?

LEARNING to Ride a Bike

So, there we were. Father and child. Training wheels removed. They're wearing more padding and body armor than a West Point grad's first day at the firing range. Their mom has warned you several times that if you hurt their baby, you will be in a far worse place than the doghouse. All you can think of is regaining some freedom from being the "dad taxi" as your little booger eater can finally travel on two wheels.

And so, you give them a little push.

Is there anything more American than learning to ride a bike? I don't know if kids in other countries even get to have bikes or not. All I know is that this is the epitome of the American spirit and experience. It's a struggle at first, as they learn their balance. Sometimes they crash, and it hurts, but they get back up and try again just like you did when you were a kid, and your parents before you. When they finally figure it out, it's one of the greatest feelings of freedom and independence that a kid can have. It also gives you yet another cherished item you can confiscate when they are being intolerable little shits. Enjoy!

Letting Boys be Boys

I'm going to focus on one gender for a little bit. Since there are only two genders it will be easy to come back to the other one, so don't worry. I've noticed in our society lately that girls are encouraged to do and be whatever they want. Frankly, this is something I have taught my daughters as well. We are now teaching girls to be their own heroes.

But we are shortchanging our boys.

It's hard to say exactly what has gone wrong, but something has. Boys are less likely to succeed in basic schooling now. As they get older, they are increasingly more likely to fall into violence and suicide than girls raised in the same homes. We tell our girls they can be whatever they want in life, but what are we telling our boys?

Call it a pendulum issue or whatever. Maybe it's that our education system is either run by women or by men who have been emasculated, but there are some in today's society trying to shame boys into being more like girls. It's freaking wrong.

I'm not saying we allow for bad behavior that is often associated with boys, like bullying (which btw, girls can be far meaner if you ask me). Basic rules of behavior still apply. I am pointing out that we have taken the role of the man in our society and diminished it. It is no longer honorable for men to be seen as the hero, the father figure, or the breadwinner. Men are now the screwups who need a woman to set them straight. Worse, in an effort to kill old stereotypes, right or wrong, we've taken away from boys the male accomplishments they once dreamed of.

Perhaps the worst thing we've taken away from boys is their fathers. More boys in America live without a positive male role model in the home now more than ever. While we view a mom as a necessity for kids, we view dads as optional. The result is a nation of mentally broken boys who end up hurting themselves or many others.

Again, I have nothing against single moms who end up in a bad situation. Some are still capable of helping a young boy learn to be a man, but it is not the same as having an actual man that the boy can and will look up to. Either purposely excluding the father or allowing the father to shirk his duty shortchanges your son. I'm sure most of the young men who end up in prison had a mom that loved them, but where the heck was their dad?

You Have Girls? God Bless You

They're so cute when they're little. If you've never had a princess look up at you with angelic eyes and call you daddy as they wrap you around their finger, you're missing out. Just don't ask me what happens when they become teenagers.

As I mentioned in the boy section, most people now tell their girls they can be whatever they want. I never excluded my daughters from anything. I encouraged both of them to go hunting and enjoy the outdoors with me whenever I could. I'll never forget seeing my oldest daughter charging up a hill, rifle in hands, trying to get a good shot at a buck that we saw. When she later joined the Air Force, I couldn't be more proud.

But letting your girls be themselves starts at a young age. It doesn't just mean you take them hunting or teach them to change the oil in your car. It means coaching them as they try to figure out what they are into. If that happens to be dolls and tea parties, refer them to their mother. I happen to have a friend, non-military, who is raising four girls and two of them are *bonus* kids (not his biologically). If a civilian can do this, you can too.

MULTIPLE KIDS

EVERYONE HAS advice on how to raise a kid. But what if you have two? Or three? I remember when we had our third kid, we realized at that point they outnumbered us. They realize this too. Just take them to the mall and they will devise a plan to run in three different directions. Sure, you'll catch two of them, but one will escape to have some fun and hide under the department store clothing racks. Because, "Fuck you Mom and Dad, this shit's fun and I really don't care if I get kidnapped by that creepy old pervert with candy."

It may seem difficult raising multiple kids, and trust me it is, but it has its advantages too. If you space them apart enough, eventually you can stick your oldest with babysitting duties. It teaches them responsibility and also acts as good birth control when they see how fucking crazy it is to be a parent.

On one occasion, my three little insurgents were having a bad day. They were fighting over the TV, over the cereal, over everything. It was like the bad attitude fairy had sprinkled an equal amount of asshole dust on each of them. So, I intervened. Now, I had been reading about non-violent intervention and how parents in fantasy dreamland never spanked their kids (they just popped Xanax and waited for their neglected little psychos to go shoot up a schoolyard). I wanted to give them each a little smack on the head to shake off the asshole dust, but I decided instead to try something new. Using my friendliest, yet still commanding voice, I instructed each of them onto the trampoline in the backyard. It had a safety net so I didn't have to worry about escapees. I then lectured them on sibling love as I washed away all the asshole dust with a garden hose. Amazingly, they forgot about all their bitchy little attitudes towards each other. It turned out to be a good day . . . for me.

Making it a Competition

As I just mentioned, boys and girls are different. They learn differently and react to their experiences differently as well. I've talked to numerous parents who are concerned with their boys' low motivation levels about school and learning, whereas they don't seem to have the same problem with their daughters. Motivating young people to learn and excel is something that drill sergeants have to tackle every day.

There's plenty of methods to motivating young troops. My boot in your ass (fear of the drill sergeant) is always fun, but I have found that turning things into a competition, where appropriate, is a great motivator that teaches teamwork and leadership as well.

Look at your son's classroom. Imagine they have a math test coming, and your son happens to hate math (or reading, pick your subject here). He avoids his homework and doesn't study for the test. To him, it doesn't matter if he passes or fails because it's just a stupid math test. Eventually, you will go talk to his female teacher, and she will tell you that he just needs to get on medication for his ADHD.

Now imagine that the teacher (one who gives a fuck) turns

tests into a competition. They break the class down into mixed teams and gives them attainable goals. The teams compete for the highest scores with an actual prize for the winners. I have done this with basic trainees and watched them motivate themselves to new heights. It will work with kids too.

The great thing about competition is that, despite what the female teachers might think, it actually does not scare off the girls. If you think young girls aren't competitive, you haven't seen a high school volleyball game. They're brutally competitive! We separate boys and girls in sports because they're built differently, but in academics it's more of a level playing field. Competition just puts learning in a language that boys can understand!

Breaking them into teams also improves the competitive experience. Now the average kid who doesn't normally ace the tests has the chance to compete with the young brainiac who never fails. The smart kid has an added incentive to help coach their teammates now as well. Army privates learn that their team is only as strong as the weakest link. And since they're not allowed to pick and chose their own platoon or team, it's up to them to help their teammate succeed. It's hard at first, but this is where you will see them pull together. Being a part of a team builds real motivation.

Marital Relations

By the time you are in this stage, you've been with your partner for more than a few years. The honeymoon is likely gone, but you may have evolved into something better. If so, count your blessings. A lot of couples don't make it past this stage. Those that do often admit that it takes work.

There's something about men after their kids are older than

four years of age. Their biology seems to tell them it's OK to take off now and go make babies somewhere else. It's believed to come from their cavemen ancestors. That's no excuse! Your cavemen ancestors also didn't stand up straight in formation or shave their nasty faces! Don't even ask if they put the seat down Private Snuffy! The point is that stepping out on your kids and family is always the wrong answer.

Not to leave women out of the equation here. I hate to tell you this, but some of you can be downright mean to your husbands. You get your dream wedding and your darling babies to post pictures of, and then you turn into angrier versions of your mother. Your husband is relegated to the garage where you still maintain control over how much beer he drinks. Worse, some of you cut off sexual relations to once a month or less. After a few years of this, your husband is likely either daydreaming of the secretary at work or of ways to kill himself. Is this really how you want to treat him? You need to lighten up a little and pay more attention to your battle buddy, sister!

If you're a woman in this situation, you can save your marriage, but you'll need to compromise a little. Schedule some alone time on your calendar, let's say every two weeks. Get the kids to a sitter, put on something nice, and start guzzling your favorite hootch. Nothing kills inhibitions faster than a few glasses of wine and some Jell-O shooters. You and your husband will have your spark back in no time.

Like I said in the previous chapter, most of these problems can be controlled by talking to each other. Notice how I didn't say "solved." The real world is never that easy, but if you communicate you can overcome a lot of issues. By communicate, I mean you have an actual conversation where you both listen to each other! Come on Snuffy! Do I have to hold your freaking hand everywhere? And when I say listen, I mean you better pay attention Snuffy, or you will, I repeat, YOU WILL GO FUCK YOURSELF.

RAISING TEENAGERS. NO, YOU CAN'T JUST SHOOT THEM.

BLUE PHASE

Forty-eight privates had come a long way, and they were starting to feel pretty confident about their chances of making it out of basic training. They had a half day to themselves, and the little piss ants decided to parade around the barracks in their dress uniforms or Class A's. It was all fun and games until the drill sergeants came back. We wanted to make them do PT in their nice, hot, dress uniforms for an hour or two, but Senior Drill intervened. We couldn't have their dress uniforms all messed up before graduation he said. How about some MOPP 4 training instead?

Now, MOPP suits are like charcoal lined coveralls that get hotter than Hades and stink from all the previous trainees who've worn them. Add to this a gas mask, rubber boots, and gloves; not only is Private Snuffy now secure from a chemical attack, he's also miserable as hell. In the words of a famous space pilot, "Don't get cocky Kid."

ALRIGHT TROOPS, YOU MADE IT THROUGH BABY PUKE and soccer balls, and now your little darlings have turned into zit-faced assholes. Congratulations, you have teenagers! This stage is like Blue Phase in basic training. You've got them trained on the basics of life, and they are almost ready to graduate and leave, if only they don't get themselves killed first.

This stage often has a lot of tension for you and your kids. I've known some drill sergeants over the years who had a tough time with their own teenagers, so it probably won't be any easier for you. If you've been there as a parent and applied any discipline into their lives, they are probably looking forward to becoming an adult and getting what they see as the ultimate freedom. If you haven't been there for them, they are likely resentful and this is going to be a real challenge for you. Either way, the restrictions may ease up, but the rules are still the same.

For explanatory purposes I consider a teenager to be in the ages of thirteen to eighteen. I realize your own kids will have different levels of maturity which will determine how hard or soft you may have to parent. Just remember that in this stage more than ever you still need rules and expectations. You are no longer the one who changes their diapers, but you are also not their new best friend.

You and your partner need to discuss the rules and discipline of your household early in this stage, and make sure that your kids know what is expected of them. Where you wouldn't let your eight-year-old hang out until midnight down at the local burger house, you might allow for different behavior for your fifteen-year-old. However, the fifteen-year-old still needs to know when is the appropriate time to be home. I knew a college football coach who insisted on his players being in by midnight (obviously on an honor system). His reasoning was that nothing good ever happens after midnight, but plenty of bad stuff does happen, and he didn't want his players getting into trouble. I would advise that you stick to a similar mindset of midnight or earlier.

Whatever rules you both decide on, you also need to determine consequences to make those rules stick. I have found that sending a teenager to their room is really not an effective manner of discipline (they'll just sleep). However, taking away their cell phone drives them freaking nuts! Taking the door off of their bedroom is another way to remind them who is in charge.

The bottom line is that teenagers are soon going to be adults, and they have to learn to be responsible. You can't hold their hand or make every decision for them. You can guide them and hopefully protect them from the big mistakes. Let them make the little mistakes though. They still need to learn.

Technology and Social Media

Speaking of cell phones, you need to discuss your child's use of these fun little gadgets. In my own household, we recently broke down and got rid of our useless land line. However, in so doing, we realized that our twelve-year-old had no way to contact us, so we got him a cell phone with some clear rules on proper use, data, texting, etc. The phone exists for our convenience and contact needs, not his. Everything else is a privilege that can be taken away.

Some parents don't believe in their kids having cell phones, and some are more liberal with them. I see it as another tool that can be used in teaching them discipline. If you didn't know already, most schools do not allow the use of cell phones during classroom hours. You can help enforce this rule with the occasional check on their use. Just log on with your service provider, and ask about this option.

Today's cell phones do more than just call and text. They're basically a small computer, which means your kid can surf the net and get into no end of trouble. Add to that a portable camera and apps like Snapchat, and you have a recipe for some pretty risqué behavior. Most of you have likely heard of Facebook being used by kids to bully and post inappropriate content. You may not know of some of the other apps out there that can be misused. I advise parents to know the passwords for all of your kid's accounts and to block apps that you do not approve of.

By the time you read this, there will likely be new apps out there that let kids do stupid shit while hiding it from you. It's your job to keep up with the times and combat this. I suggest finding a kid you are not related too and bribing them for help.

One of the main things you need to remember at all times with your teen is that they are legally still children, and you can label them that way until the day they leave. "Young Adult" is a term they need to earn, not one that is given. Keep control of your kids, or they will gain control of you.

There's something else about social media. You may have noticed a lot of adults are addicted to it now as well. Look at any room full of your peers when they're on break. They are probably staring at their cell phones. Our society has an addiction to social media now, for better or worse. Eventually, someone smarter than me will come up with a solution. For now, if you value your sanity, along with your children's, I suggest you take a look at this problem and at least set some ground rules.

Dating

I'M GOING to open up a can o' worms here and give you my un-humble opinion (I'm a drill sergeant: my opinion is never humble). No dating for teenagers. Should I speak louder? NO DATING! Was that clear enough for you?

OK, now take a deep breath. Go ahead and yell at me or

come up with all of your arguments and excuses for why your little hormonal twit should be out dry-humping in the back of a car by the local high school. Does that make you feel better? Good, because my rule still stands, and if you don't like it go fuck yourself.

Call me a hypocrite or an asshole, I really don't care. I don't allow teenagers to date. Your parents may have allowed it. Mine certainly did. But I am saying no. To me, youth is something that should be treasured. As parents, we should not seek to turn our babies into little porn stars, but we should instead encourage them to enjoy being young while they can. There's plenty of time for dating when they turn eighteen.

Think about it. Do you remember a lot of healthy relationships in high school? From what I've seen most of them were filled with drama, emotional abuse, and the risks of teen pregnancy. There's no real benefit that I can see to letting teens date. Let your kids be kids. Let them have friends and enjoy a life without the pressure of dating. When they're eighteen they might still make mistakes, but at least at that point they are more mature and will have a better chance of getting things right.

Sexual Relations

OK, since we're on the subject of dating (I said No, didn't I?), I suppose we need to talk about sex and kids. In my not so fucking humble opinion, sex and kids are two words that should not go together. I know, your grandma had three kids by the time she was thirteen all while her husband was fighting WWII and those kids turned out just fine. Sort of. But this isn't 1940 Bucko. They have laws against that shit now.

I believe my generation (at least the half of us with active brain cells) have become a lot better at sheltering our children. We know all the tricks from our childhood, and we provide enough digital entertainment that most of our kids never leave the house anyway. The problem is, our kids are more dependent now. An eighteen-year-old American now is less qualified to raise a child than probably at any point in our history.

While our kids are less qualified to raise babies, our society is pushing sex at them faster than ever before. They literally have porn, adult chat rooms, sexting, Game of Thrones, and everything else at their fingertips every minute of the day on their phones and TV. There is no getting around the sexualized culture unless you lock them in a padded room with no WiFi. Which most of you aren't going to do. So now what?

Obviously, at some point, you have to have the talk about sex and pregnancy because those two go together. It may be a smart thing to tell them that sex can be fun, but it makes babies, and it's really not for children. Some of you will run out and put your kids on birth control, which I don't necessarily agree with, but that's your call. Some of you will just let the school handle this through sex education. Frankly, if they do this for teens in a way that advises abstinence, I'm OK with it. But when the morons start teaching six-year-olds about gender pronouns and how to have anal sex you know, we have a problem. You should probably intervene and get a new school.

DRIVING

IT'S another classic memory of most kids and parents. That wonderful time when they turn sixteen, and you get to ride white-knuckled in the passenger seat as they careen through multiple near-death experiences learning how to fricking drive. Hooahh.

This is another area where my opinion might not jive with yours. Just so you know, the leading cause of death for teenagers in America is not sex, drugs, and rock and roll. It's also not guns. The leading cause of death for young people is motor vehicles (not to offend you equality types, but the death rate is also higher for boys than girls).

Now you will have to make your own decision here. In the old days, teens were given the privilege of driving because a lot of them had jobs and needed to get to work. Nowadays the minimum wage rules pretty much rule out teens from getting a job, so you likely don't have to deal with this. Chances are your teen really wants to drive, and you may not like always being their personal taxi, so it's up to you. You're the parent. You have the right to decide if your child is mature enough to get behind the wheel or not. Driving is a privilege and not a right. It's certainly not owed to anyone. If you decide not to let them drive until they're older, they'll get over it.

Picking Your Battles

Raising kids and going to war do have some similarities. When sizing up a fight, it's important to ask if that particular hill is worth dying on or not. A lot of parenting experts seem to emphasize this. There are times when you're going to have disagreements with your teenagers. The trick here is that you want to instill a sense of responsibility in them, and that sometimes means letting them make their own mistakes.

What areas do you let them make their own decisions?

This is where I look back to basic training and ask myself, what are the basic standards? Private Snuffy is required to pass the PT test (Physical Training for you civilian types) and qualify with his rifle. There's no requirement that he excel, just that he has to pass. Sometimes passing is good enough for certain privates; however, there are others who are letting themselves down with a passing score because they have the potential for so much better.

This is something you can pass on to your kids. Let them know, based on their abilities, what you expect in regards to their grades and performance. Not all kids were meant to go to MIT no matter how hard you push them, but all kids have the potential to be great at something, even Private Snuffy.

The next thing I would point out is to look at the permanency of what your child wants to do. A tattoo on the neck or face is pretty permanent. It also looks freaking stupid as hell and will almost guarantee your little derelict will never get hired for anything over minimum wage. As a parent, I say no to all tattoos for anyone under eighteen. I also maintain strict control over piercings, because some piercings do leave marks (and stretched out ears) that are hard to explain later.

Wearing weird clothes is a lot less permanent, and hair grows back too. So long as they're not overly sexual, this an area where you can give your kids some personal choice. If they want to be laughed at by society, let them knock themselves out. I would advise against slogans like "Fuck the Police" though, as they are still in your house and always need to maintain some basic respect. If you happen to wear shirts like that, go back and read chapter one again. Then punch yourself in the face, hippy.

Hair color is another way they now express themselves. And you know what? I love it. My oldest teen went through this and dyed her hair purple. She made her own decision and stuck with it for a while. Eventually, she grew tired of it and colored her hair back to its natural color. I didn't tell her no on this one. I let her make her own decision and take responsibility for any consequences, of which there were none. Hair can be colored over and over. If it's cut off or into some weird shape, it grows back. This is a great area to let your teens have some personal control.

CLOTHING

SINCE I MENTIONED CLOTHING, I'll further address it here. While teenagers do like to wear stuff that pushes the envelope, this is a good time to teach them about dressing for success. They want to be non-conformist by wearing whatever the current fad is. Your job is to teach them what the real adult world will expect of them if they want a job that doesn't involve picking up trash on the side of the freeway.

Every young man should own some nicer clothes and know how to wear them. Start him out with some pleated khakis, a buttoned shirt, and maybe even a sport coat. Girls should likewise have some more professional attire. These kinds of clothes used to be called your *Sunday best*, but you can wear them on Tuesday if it makes you happy. Even if they don't wear these clothes all the time, it's important to have a set handy, and teach them how to dress properly. It probably wouldn't hurt some of you knuckleheads to have some professional attire either.

Young people should stay away from sexualized clothes as much as possible. Boys do not need to wear pants that sag and show off their underwear. In fact, call me an old fart, but nothing pisses me off more than dudes with their asses hanging out of their pants! Girls do not need shorts that let their butt cheeks hang out either. I'm assuming you are raising decent future adults and not strippers, right? You are the parent it is your job to enforce the rules of proper apparel! I enforce the double standard, and I often told my daughters that if it was something I would want to see their mother in it probably wasn't appropriate for them. Teach your kids some class, and let them show their individuality by being high achievers. There's a novel fucking idea.

Drugs & Alcohol

I'VE DISCUSSED THIS EARLIER, but mostly about your use of chemical escape. For your kids, it should be a no brainer that you do not let them partake in drugs and alcohol. Just say no.

Obviously, with teens, this is harder than it sounds. They probably have more access to illegal drugs at their high school than you have on Saturday night with your friends. In fact, one of your friends likely has a drug dealer from your kids' school on speed dial right now.

Then you have the hippies trying to legalize marijuana. I'm not arguing for or against this, but these jackasses will come out with every argument you can think of about how great weed is and how it's practically a wonder drug. All so they can smoke it and get high. The problem is your kids will hear these arguments, and some kids are just stupider than others when it comes to drugs. Prolonged use of marijuana messes with the brain. It is also still a gateway drug to the worse shit, like methamphetamine. When your kid starts using meth, it's usually too late to save them. You will be the crying mom posting a reward for your stolen shit when everyone else in town knows it's your loser son.

It's your job as the parent to put your foot down. You may have to inspect them when they come home late. You will need to search their rooms once in a while. **Trust but verify** is a good phrase. When you have lost a family member to drug use (like I have), you will understand how horrible that shit is, and you will want to do everything to protect your children from it, even if it pisses them off. They can still make mistakes when they grow up, but not under your roof. Are we fucking clear on this? Do you know what you can do if you don't like my opinion? That's right! Go Fuck Yourself! You're getting good at this shit!

FITNESS

"I'M ALL ABOUT FITNESS. Fitness whole pizza in my mouth!"

If you went easy on them in the previous stage (like I did), you need to really pay attention here. Unhealthy teenagers grow into unhealthy adults pretty fast. They grow into big fatties that can't serve their country or outrun zombies. They get picked on by bullies and never picked for the prom. Worse, they clog up stairways at movies and sporting events.

You have no excuse for raising an unhealthy teenager. While they may not know that a diet of frozen burritos, cookies, and soda is actually not good for them, you should freaking know better! Once again, they probably learned this behavior from you, so now is a good time to get off your damn couch and do some crunches. A hundred of them should do for now.

Stop buying frozen foods for them. Cut down on pasta products. Buy more fruits and vegetables. A better diet is a good start, but then you also need to get them exercising. It's not easy, but if you love them, you will do it.

Your kids' fitness is related to your own. Not only are they your kids (hopefully), and share your DNA, but they learn from your fitness habits as well. If you are a couch potato, they are likely to follow. So, don't be.

I know scheduling in this day and age is really difficult. To be honest, it sucks, but you have to make it happen. Take a look at your next weekend and theirs. Tell them to cancel hanging out at the mall with their friends. You can forgo watching a full day of mind-numbing sports or internet surfing as well. Do a little research, and find a hiking trail near you, and take your kids on a freaking hike hippy, or swimming somewhere other than your backyard pool.

I have a really great memory of a hunting trip I took with my oldest daughter. She was probably about fifteen, and our relationship had been very difficult in those years. She was headstrong and independent and didn't want dad telling her what to do. But she was excited that we could go on our own deer hunting trip, and so was I.

It was towards the end of the season, and we hadn't had much luck before. A storm was moving in, and the forest came alive with movement. We saw a lot of deer that day, and I'll never forget the energy with which she ran up the mountain chasing a buck and firing her rifle in vain (moving targets are hard folks).

We sat and ate our lunch overlooking a nice valley that day. No fighting, just reminiscing and enjoying our time. She was finally successful that evening and killed her first deer just before dark. This made for dragging it back to the vehicle more difficult. We had to overcome some terrain obstacles, which we did together and as a team. For that one beautiful day, the bond between father and child could never be stronger. I won't tell you that we never disagreed after that, but we also fought a lot less. Take your kids out hunting, or fishing, or something. Just get out there and do it.

* * *

Control Your Anger

Teenagers can be trying on your patience. They really can. It doesn't matter if they're male or female, they all tend to get a case of the attitude at some point. They've also had years of studying you and learning how to push your buttons, but they don't have the wisdom to know when they've gone too far. This is when it can get ugly.

I'll be the first to admit that I used to yell a lot. When my authority is challenged, I turn up the volume, and I will be heard. What I've learned with kids though, is that sometimes you have to let things simmer down rather than heat up. Kids can be emotional, and they reach a boiling point like a teapot. When you see this happening, try to just let them have their moment. Let them yell and scream and cry and then they can go to their room. Try talking with them calmly once they've calmed down. If they broke the rules, you can still explain the consequences an hour later.

Mind you, if they get violent or start breaking things, you need to step in and put a stop to that shit immediately! If you're a single mom (didn't I advise against this?) and your teenage son is bigger than you, you had better find a way to get him under control. If he harms you and gets away with it, he will likely hurt other women down the road; our society generally looks down on that. If you can't bring yourself to taser his ass, find a friend who lifts weights to smack some sense into him. Just do it with love and not anger.

When our kids lose control, we tend to as well. If you see your spouse starting to lose it, try to diffuse the situation. Drill Sergeants routinely help out their battle buddies when they see the scary temper come out. Sure, we may watch them smoke Private Snuffy until tears are coming out of his eyes, but if it gets out of line, we'll let our battle buddy know he's got an "important phone call in the staff office." You and your spouse probably already know what *safe* words are (you dirty freaks). Develop one for dealing with your kids.

Remember that when you let your temper take control, you're giving your kids an element of control over you. They will learn how to press your buttons in search of this response. You have to develop the self-control and discipline not to let this happen. Take the buttons away from them, and they will stop trying to press them.

Preparing Them for Adulthood.

They've almost made it, and so have you. But has anyone figured out what comes next? Are they going to college, learning a trade, or maybe they want to be total American badasses like me and join the military? You might want to have this conversation with them before they graduate. Otherwise you might find out that your son's dream was just to stay with you and play video games the rest of his life, and your daughter is planning to make babies with a crater-faced drug dealer and get on welfare.

Remember this phrase: **Proper Planning and Practice Prevents Piss Poor Performance.** No good mission gets carried out without a plan first, so you've got to have a plan! Take a look at your kid. Are they smart? They're probably going to college. Are they not so book smart but good with their hands? They're trade school bound. They're any of the above, but you can't figure out how to pay for the schooling? Uncle Sam has you covered folks. Kids today can earn a lot of money for school while serving our great nation in the armed forces.

Now, I may be a drill sergeant, but I'm a dad too. I used to think that if I re-enlisted multiple times, I could pay off not only my own debt to our country but my children's as well. There would be no need for them to serve since I did it for so long. I also knew I did not want my kids going into the Army if I could help it. I was determined that their lives would be better than mine.

Then my oldest daughter came up with a compromise we could both live with. She was joining the military not only to pay for college, but to serve her country too. Being smarter than her dad though, she was going Air Force. The Air Force is almost like the real military, but with better food, softer beds, and cable TV. Damn, why didn't I think of that?

BE THEIR PARENT, not their friend.

I SEE this attitude with parents and their kids more and more these days. Maybe it's a product of millennials and their fear of confrontation. Maybe it's a product of our digital society. Everyone is so cut off from other human beings that they fear losing their children's love more than losing disciplinary control. What's surprising to me is that I see it happening with parents who claim to believe you should be their parent, not their friend. Paying lip service to parenting catch phrases doesn't work folks!

What exactly do I mean by being their parent and not their friend? Am I instructing you to address them as hippies and scumbags and avoid hugs until they're 18? Not unless you want them to hate you (Asshole). It's about maintaining boundaries. You love your children. You give them hugs and praise, and yes, sometimes you spoil them when you can (a little). But you always maintain the boundary line of who is in control. You always make sure that your rules are being followed above all else. Homework and chores get done before recreation. Family dinners are not to be blown off. And at all times, respect from your children is mandatory.

Now, we all have different sets of rules that we feel our children need to adhere too. Whatever those rules may be, you need to maintain them. When you don't, you will lose their respect. They may still love you, but they won't respect you. This is where you start to become their friend and are no longer an authority figure to them. This is when it starts to go bad.

You see, even when I was a drill sergeant, I had a boss. My 1st Sergeant was my boss. Not my friend. I didn't love him. Some days, I fucking hated him, but I always respected him. His word was law, and I made sure not to cross that. This was necessary for the order of the company and the training of all the insane little Private Snuffies we had to deal with. If my 1st Sergeant had decided he wanted to be my friend, or worse, a friend to the trainees, he would have lost our respect. Even worse, he'd have lost control, and training would have failed. Fortunately, I never saw this happen.

I've seen plenty of parents lose control though. Maybe you've heard the line "I'd rather my kids drink at home with me than out at a party somewhere." Or, "They're going to have sex anyway, so I put my 14-year-old on birth control." These are the boundary lines you should really reconsider crossing, or next it will be "Well, his friends are all thugs, so I bought him a ski mask to help protect his identity on his next mugging." Here's a novel idea. How about we stop enabling our kids' bad decisions and start setting our expectations just a little higher?

I've also seen the results of friending your kids. It usually ends in teen pregnancy or drinking and drug problems before they're even 18. I've seen parents nearly lose their kids to drunk driving. It's fucking heartbreaking. But worst of all, is seeing the parents make excuses for their kids. If you won't listen to me, look at their stories. Look at how you raise your kids, and fix your shit before you lose them. A kid who doesn't respect you or your rules probably also does not respect themselves. If you really love them, be their fucking parent, and show them you care enough to say NO. They already have friends, and those are a dime a dozen. A real parent is priceless. <u>Be one.</u>

Marital Relations

If you've made it this far, at this point, your marriage is pretty rock solid. You really don't need an army drill sergeant to tell you how to keep it real in your sex life, do you? By now you've either got that figured out and have a routine, or one of you goes out with friends a lot while the other keeps the local liquor store in business. I hope you've figured out the former.

One thing to watch out for is the dreaded midlife crisis. It tends to hit men more than women and happens around forty. When your former dream boy's six-pack has turned into a pony keg, and he grows a beard to compensate for the bald patch on top of his head, you may see some strange behavior. Don't worry. He just needs that sports car to attract women half his age so that he can feel young again. What's the worst that can happen?

On second thought, help your husband out with this. Get him that video game system he's been wanting. Send the kids to Grandma's and wear that cheerleader costume for him. If that doesn't work, load him up on enough cheeseburgers and beer to put him in a food coma until the crisis passes. If he lives, he may thank you later.

SO, YOU RAISED PERFECT KIDS, NOW WHAT?

There was Private Joe Snuffy, fresh out of basic training having his first free weekend at AIT with a couple of buddies. They were dressed back on the block in full thug attire, baggy pants and all. They had just scored some hooch from the class 6 with help from an older student. They were laughing all the way into the parking lot when a truck pulled up with the last three people they ever wanted to see. Two of their basic training Drill Sergeants along with their new AIT instructor were looking at the underage dipshits with two cases of beer and a bottle of whiskey. Joe Snuffy's fun was over, and his new shitstorm had begun.

IF YOU'RE READING THIS AS YOU RAISE KIDS, THIS chapter may seem completely ridiculous. You're thinking to yourselves, "What do you mean? Now what, Drill Sergeant? It's time to PARTAY!!!" Mom's got the daughter's room decked out with more sewing and scrapbooking material than a Southern Baptist yard sale. Dad put a hot tub on the back porch with a sign that reads NO SWIMSUITS ALLOWED. At this point, who in the hell needs a Drill Sergeant?

OK, you got me. Scrapbooking and nudist living sounds like a total blast (freaks), but you're not out of the woods yet. With today's economy your kids may choose to attend college close to home, AND THEN STAY WITH YOU! If you have multiple kids, by the time your youngest leaves the house, your oldest could suddenly come back home. They may have just discovered that a doctorate in philosophy still only qualifies you for a job flipping burgers and taking orders from last year's journalism major. Even worse, they could return bearing offspring. If this happens, I would love to tell you that childproofing your home works, but I've found that the little buggers do just keep getting back in!

When They Go Bad

THIS IS a difficult issue that too many parents go through. Some kids just don't turn out right. Whether you were there to hold their hand constantly or they were a typical latchkey kid, some of them will make bad choices. They will hang with the wrong crowd and get into drugs and other self-destructive behavior, and it will be by their own choice. If you've honestly done the best you could as a parent, this will still hurt you, but you'll have to let your little assholes make their own mistakes. Think back to your own youth and ask yourself if you would have listened to your own parents? Even if you say yes (liar), your kids are their own people who will make their own decisions.

I've seen this happen a lot in my generation. Almost always, it is drug use that steals them away. Often there are psychological issues and pain they are dealing with that makes them turn to the drugs, but sometimes it is the drugs that cause the mental issues. Either way, it rarely ends well, and it brings a lot of pain for the family. Its why we see a lot of older couples now raising their grandkids. It's a reminder to all of us, to spend time with your kids while they are young. Stop making excuses for them, and get them away from the bad influences that are out there. When all else fails, pray.

If Your Kids Join the Military

When my oldest told me that she was joining the military I had mixed emotions. Sure, as a dad I was very proud of her for making that sacrifice for her country, but I also know how tough the military can be. For many years I felt that I was doing my duty so that one day my kids wouldn't have too. Even worse, I was still in the Reserves at the time she was enlisting. Now, my job took on even new levels of responsibility for me.

In the end, her mother and I had to accept that this was her decision. America is her country too, and she wanted to give back to this nation before going out and pursuing her own dreams. I can tell you now that it hasn't always been easy for her, but she is doing fine. Your kids sleep safer at night because my kid is helping protect them.

Enough about my Air Force brat. Let's talk about your little booger eaters becoming future Joe Snuffies. Some of you parents (and by parents, I mean moms), get a little dramatic over what happens to your kids in the military. Please understand that drill sergeants are not evil monsters (more like professional assholes). They are there to take your weak, inept, useless, civilian crybaby child and turn them into a strong, capable, American fighting machine.

So, when your son or daughter writes home and complains about how we are treating them, I urge you, resist the temptation to call our Company office and complain about it, because not only will it NOT help improve their situation, but (trust me on this) it will make it worse. If you didn't want their drill sergeants to pick on them, you shouldn't have held them so close to your damn bosom and let them be fucking adults! But no worries. Where you failed, rest assured drill sergeants will not. When we are done with them, they can handle anything this world has to throw at them. You really should thank us, and send cookies.

Helicopter and Lawnmower Parents

Alright, listen up. Some of you parents are complete jerkwads when it comes to the success of your children. It started with Little League baseball. Yes, we've all seen you there, screaming at the umpire, or worse, at your child, all because you didn't chase your dream of being the star player, and now you want to live through them.

Look, we all want our kids to do well. We want them to succeed in life, be happy and have friends, and all that shit, but you have to let them learn this stuff on their own! Don't be the helicopter parent who follows you kid through college and everywhere else, ready to scoop them up should they stumble and actually need your sorry ass again. They'll be fine. They got this!

As if helicopter parents weren't bad enough, now there are lawnmower parents. Where helicopter parents hover in case they need to coach their kids on how to do something better, lawnmower parents come in to do everything for their kids to ensure success. That means doing their homework, buying them friends, and yes, mowing their freaking lawns.

Take a minute here and think back. Can you imagine how fucking annoying it would have been if your parents had done this shit to you? Back the fuck off people! Let your kids make mistakes and go without occasionally. Let them learn what it's like to NOT be able to afford something they want! It will teach them to follow a budget. If you're loaded and need to spoil someone, just wait for the grandkids. That's when it's really fun.

Adoption & Foster Kids

This section literally could have gone anywhere in this book. At some point in your adult life you may be considering adoption, or taking in foster children. I urge you to give foster parenting some consideration.

There are a lot of screwed up people out there. Some total shit-for-brains assholes and complete dope-head losers who have pissed away their opportunities in life. As far as I'm concerned, most of them can just go play in traffic. Sadly, however, they have left behind children who have done nothing wrong save being born by the wrong parents.

These are the kids that need your help. In the year I spent working in foster care, I learned that there are no happy stories when it comes to foster children. Often, their parents are either dead or deserve to be. It leaves the children with a lot of pain and psychological trauma.

You can help. You can be the guiding force in a kid's life that steers them away from the bad choices of their parents. Perhaps, now that your kids are out of the house, you even have room for them.

It won't be easy. You will need to dig deep and find your inner drill sergeant, and channel the shit out of him. Kids in this situation often need a very firm hand to keep them in line. You will need extreme patience, and the ability to recognize when you are in over your head.

Still, you can do this. Many others before you have done

this. Consider it just another obstacle in life for you to adapt to and overcome. But first, get training. Find out about the different levels of screwed up that some kids can be. Take some classes on how to best help these children. Prepare yourself for the worst, and you may end up pleasantly surprised by the best. In the end, a hundred years from now, it won't matter how nice your house was or how much money you had, but it will matter that you made a difference in the life of a child.

Who knows? Maybe they'll even grow up to be a badass drill sergeant.

IN CLOSING

I CAN TELL YOU, TRUTHFULLY, THAT EVEN WHEN YOUR kids leave and even if it's not to go sell drugs on a street corner, you will still worry about them. You will still want to help them through all of life's trials that you know they will go through. Whether they join the military or not, you will worry about their safety. If they move far away, you will miss them all the time. If you did your job as a parent and followed even half of what I've been telling you in this book, they will miss you too.

Your job doesn't end when your kids move out. Even if they go on to become rich and famous and cure cancer, they're going to need you. The world has become a complicated place, with a lot of gray area when it comes to moral values. As an older parent or grandparent, it's increasingly important that you stick around and share your wisdom with the younger generations. Run for your local school board. Volunteer with a local firehouse or National Guard unit. Don't just hop in your RV and check out. Be involved. If you were ever a service member, I really do insist.

Just remember, no matter what anyone else tells you about raising your kids, they're your kids. You're the one who is responsible for them. You're the one who's in charge. You should also remember that, however you decide to raise them, it's the time you put in that will really matter the most. It's the memories you make with them that will affect them the most. Your time with them will go by very fast, so I hope you stop to enjoy it. You'll have plenty of time to rest when they've left the house (or when you're dead). Get your ass out of bed and take your kids fishing.

One of the most amazing things for me has been to see how different my own three children turned out. They each have their own preferences and personalities. They have their own work ethic and approach to life. Sure, they get a lot of it from myself and their mother, but they became their own people. I'm so proud of them for this, and I love them more than anything. I don't ever regret being their dad. Not for a second.

I hope that this book has helped you with your kids, and that you're fortunate enough to watch them grow into good people. We live in one of the rare places on earth where our children can go out and achieve whatever they put their minds too.

I also hope you won't forget the men and women of our armed services who protect your children's freedom to seek out their dreams. If one or more of your children, or you for that matter, are serving in our nation's military, you have my utmost respect.

Thank you again for reading my book. I appreciate your support, and I look forward to writing more guides like this. We live in the greatest nation on earth, and it's so amazing to me that I get to do this. So, thank you, and may God bless you and your family.

And if you see Private Snuffy, tell him I said to go fuck himself.

ACKNOWLEDGMENTS

A funny thing happened on the way to publishing the book you're reading. I had written the first draft, when I got an offer to work in Boise, Idaho. It was an amazing career builder for me, but it meant living away from my family for at least a year. Soon after, I found myself in divorce talks with my wife of twenty years. When you go through such life-changing events, things like finishing a book get put aside along with other potential dreams. A year passed while I tried to figure out my life and future.

Along my journey, I found a new editor in the Boise area. Stacey Smekofske worked diligently to take my writing and hone it into something that looks professional. I also found Jane Dixon-Smith, a cover artist from the UK with a real talent for making books look sharp and presentable.

As a US Army Drill Sergeant, my job was sometimes to be a complete asshole. It was also to be a teacher and a mentor to the brave young men and women who voluntarily took the oath to defend our beautiful nation. I learned much from them, and I hope they and their families all know how much I appreciate the sacrifices they made for all of us. America is a beacon of hope for peace and freedom in the world. Those who have never served rarely understand the truth of this.

On completion of this book, I am back in Northern California and living with my wife and our kids again. There is nothing perfect about our marriage, but she still supports my ideas and my writing. She helped with the final formatting and publishing of this book. It is why, aside from God, she is always the one who deserves my highest thanks and gratitude. She is a great parent because she is a great person.

I couldn't possibly write a parenting book without also thanking my children. Without them, I wouldn't have all the hilarious stories that every parent knows so well. I wouldn't have a clue how to tell other people how they should raise their kids. I would probably have more cash in my wallet, but I still love them.

Finally, thank you to my readers. It is for you that I endeavor to live up to higher standards and give you my very best. I appreciate each and every one of you.

Hooah.

ABOUT STEVEN THOMPSON

Steven J. Thompson is a prolific author who grew up in Northern California. While he has worked for years in the fields of politics, foster care, and advocacy for victim's rights, writing has always been a passion of his. In 2015, Steven wrote his debut book, *The Daughters Daring*, which he dedicated to his daughters. He was inspired by the countless bedtime stories he told them when they were little. Steven also enjoys writing poetry, and recently published *The Drill Sergeant's Guide to Parenting*, which includes hilarious stories from both his military career and raising children.

When he's not immersed in writing and work, Steven likes to fish, hunt, and being in the great outdoors. Most importantly, he loves to spend quality time with his three children. Steven is a veteran who also served over ten years as an Army Reserve Drill Sergeant. He received his degree from Chico State University.

facebook.com/SJThompsonBooks

www.ingramcontent.com/pod-product-compliance
Lightning Source LLC
Chambersburg PA
CBHW031410040426
42444CB00005B/507